DISCOVER HIDDEN SECRET WISDOM

A RECREATIONAL THERAPIST'S SYSTEM ON HOW YOU CAN BECOME GREAT AT ANYTHING

DANNY PETTRY, MS, CTRS

www.HiddenSecretWisdom.com/bonus

MW01222622

DISCOVER HIDDEN SECRET WISDOM.
A Recreational Therapist's System on
How You Can Become Great at Anything

Self-Published by:
Danny Pettry's Independent Education for the Recreational
Therapist, LLC. Beckley, West Virginia 25801-2001.
USA. Online: www.DannyPettry.Com

Copyright © 2009 by Danny Pettry, II, MS, CTRS. All rights
reserved. Printed in the United States of America. No part of
this book may be used or reproduced in any manner
whatsoever without written permission except in the case of
brief quotations embodied in critical articles or reviews. For
information, email: Danny@dannypettry.com

Library Publication Data

Pettry, II, Danny W.
          Discover hidden secret wisdom: a recreational
therapist's system on how you can become great at anything. /
Danny W. Pettry, II, MS, CTRS

ISBN 1442105739
EAN-13 9781442105737

Self-Help/ Personal Growth/ Success

Printed in the United States of America.

Limit of Liability/ Disclaimer Notice: While Danny Pettry
has used his best efforts in preparing this book; he makes no
representations or warranties with the respect to accuracy or
completeness of the contents and specifically disclaims any
implied warranties. The advice contained within this book
may not be suitable for your situation. You should consult
with a professional where appropriate. The author, Danny
Pettry shall not be liable for any loss of profit or commercial
damages, including but not limited to special, incidental,
consequential, or other damages.

Front Cover Graphic:
Magic Book © Kamaga. Rights to use received from *Can
Stock Photo*. Kamaga is a freelance graphic designer and
illustrator located in Warsaw, Poland.

Get Two Copies of This Book

Get one for yourself & one for a friend. Give this book to anyone you care about. It is a great gift for high school graduates, too.

Buy Online: www.HiddenSecretWisdom.Com

To:
_____

From:
_____

Date:
_____

Message:
_____

_____

_____

_____

_____

_____

_____

Acclaim for Danny Pettry's 1ˢᵗ Bestseller

This book was ranked #50 in bestselling self-help > success books on Amazon.Com on Sept. 22, 2009.

"In the early 1980's I had the privilege of attending the Leisure and Aging Institute at *Olgebay Park,* West Virginia. The late great Dr. Fred Humphrey presented a session on "Therapeutic Use of the Self." Dr. Humphrey suggested that recreation therapists must focus on taking care of one self so that he or she can become a better care giver or therapist. Danny Pettry has captured this concept in his book, *Discover Hidden Secret Wisdom: A Recreational Therapist's System on How you Can Become Great at Anything.*

Danny brings passion to his work and to his life and he wants to share this with all recreation therapists. Danny's words help re-energize and motivate. Each chapter is a prescription towards wellness, success, happiness, and greatness.

Even if you are just getting started as a recreation therapist or even if you are a seasoned therapist this book is for you. It will guide you on your path towards self-growth and help you become a great recreation therapist."

- **Charlie Dixon, MS, CTRS**
Operates *TR Directory Online*
www.recreationtherapy.com

Please note that this book isn't just for therapists. This book is for anyone who is seeking to reveal their own greatness and to be her (or his) best.

"I feel immense pride that one of my former students would write a book to inspire people toward self-fulfillment. He is an avid reader who wishes others to join him as avid readers. He believes reading is a key to personal growth. His writing suggests he has read numerous books on a wide variety of topics. He does an excellent job of weaving together personal experiences and examples from a wide variety of sources ranging from self-help authors to scientific researchers. He offers good common sense advice. There are many practical tips presented throughout the book. Danny is wise beyond his years. I think readers will find Danny's book a captivating approach to self-discovery."

- Professor Emeritus David Austin, Ph.D.
Indiana University
http://rt-blog.blogspot.com

"Danny Pettry's book, *Discover Hidden Secret Wisdom: A Recreational Therapist's System on How You Can Become Great at Anything* is required reading for anyone looking to jump start their positive outlook! You can't help but to have a "can do" attitude after you sit down with Danny's book! I have been able to incorporate so much of it in my work with teenagers, as well as learn a great deal for myself. There is something to motivate everyone!"

- Heather Wyman, BA, BHCII
Creative Arts Therapist
www.myspace.com/6degreesnj

"While it is true there is a plethora of self-help and wisdom building books on the market, I highly recommend *Discover Hidden Secret Wisdom,* which is truly a unique and comprehensive tool to help any individual uncover and discover their greatness. I could not put it down. I felt truly inspired by the stories, activities and resources included in the book. Don't miss out."

- **Dr. Jeanine**
Life Coach for Women Worldwide
www.simplydivinesolutions.com

"Danny Pettry's book, *Discover Hidden Secret Wisdom: A Recreational Therapist's System on How You Can Become Great at Anything,* is simply and irresistibly inspiring. Recreational Therapists, Activity Professionals, as well as other allied health professionals will feel connected to the book; however it is cleverly written for anyone who wants to achieve greatness. Pettry draws the reader in with wonderful examples, personal exercises, quotes and humor. This self-help book makes me want to go out and change the world!"

- **Kim Grandal BA, CTRS, ACC**
Director of *Re- Creative Resources, Inc*
www.recreativeresources.com

"Reading your book will help people 'Live Out Loud' for sure."

- **Logan Olson**
Creative Director of *Logan Magazine*
www.loganmagazine.com

Danny's book is so easy to read even a teenager could read it.

Advanced copies of this book were given to 100s teenagers. Here is what some of them had to say:

> "The book inspires me to get up and do something with my life."
>
> **- Hannah, age 16**

> "This book is inspirational and moving. I'd recommend this book to anyone who wants to be happier and more successful."
>
> **- Mandy, age 16**

> "Fantastic, I'd recommend this book to anyone."
>
> **- Andrew, age 18**

> "I think this book will help anyone if they choose to use the information."
>
> **- David, age 15**

> "Excellent! The book is well written and full of helpful information."
>
> **- Sarah, age 15**

> "This book is very informative. It shares wisdom on success."
>
> **- Chris, age 17**

Send Me Your Stories

Have you read one of those life-changing books or seen an inspirational movie? Have any books or movies inspired you to take action and change your life. If so, I want to know about it. Email the title of the book or movie and a story about how it has impacted your life. It can be any type of book or movie (an example: graphic novel, self-help book, fiction, non-fiction, religious, picture book, text book, or children's book) or (science-fiction movie, true story, documentary, or anything inspiring).

If it made a difference in your life then tell me about it. What secret wisdom did you gain as a result of reading the book or watching the movie?

Your story could be featured in a second edition to this book. I look forward to hearing from you.

Email: Danny@dannypettry.com

Be sure to include the following in your email:

1. The title of the book or movie
2. A story about how it inspired you
3. Your name
4. Age
5. Complete address because my team may write you to request permission to reprint/ publish your story in a second version of this book.

First Book Partnership

Buy This Book and You'll Help Kids

Notice: It's not about the book. It's about the mission. The goal of my book, *Discover Hidden Secret Wisdom* is to promote the #1 skill needed to become great. That skill is literacy. Books are filled with wisdom that you won't discover unless you read them. Many children in the world do not live in homes with age-appropriate books for them to read. A portion of the profits made from this book will benefit the non-profit First Book.

First Book provides new books to children in need addressing one of the most important factors affecting literacy – access to books. An innovative leader in social enterprise, First Book has distributed more than 65 million free and low cost books in thousands of communities. First Book now has offices in the U.S. and Canada. For more information about First Book, please visit www.firstbook.org or call 866-393-1222.

Special Permissions

I'd like to acknowledge Jonny Hawkins here. He is an amazing cartoonist who granted me permission to reprint six of his cartoons in this book.

Don't spoil the ending for me. © Jonny Hawkins. All rights reserved. This cartoon is featured in the introduction.

Inner peace. © Jonny Hawkins. All rights reserved. This cartoon is featured in chapter 3.

Do teachers still get paid? © Jonny Hawkins. All rights reserved. This cartoon is featured in chapter 5.

It doesn't work on that, son. © Jonny Hawkins. All rights reserved. This cartoon is featured in chapter 6.

Dad, can I borrow the keys to happiness? © Jonny Hawkins. All rights reserved. This cartoon is featured in chapter 7.

Give of my time. © Jonny Hawkins. All rights reserved. This cartoon is featured in chapter 10.

You can contact Jonny Hawkins by email to buy rights to his cartoons: jonnyhawkins2nz@yahoo.com

This book is dedicated to my nephew:

Gage Christopher Pettry.

Special Acknowledgements

I would like to acknowledge four groups of people who have helped me with this book.

These groups include: my team who directly assisted me with marketing, my family, the patients who I serve, and the recreational therapists who have trained me.

Group # 1: My team: Several people assisted me with this book. They deserve acknowledgements. I couldn't have completed this book without them.

Here is a list of people who helped with the promotion of my book by giving a special bonus article or e-book: David Rilkin, Margaret Merrill, Jill Schoenberg, Gerry Hopman, Suzann Rye, Brenda Herzog, Dr. Jeanine, Michael Lee, Thomas Herold, Sherry Lynn Simoes, Marie Barrett, Heather Step, Jennifer Reed, Anke Otto-Wolf, Robert Britt, Debra Beck, Cucan Pemo, Suzanne Roloff, Anne Stewart, Sami Wnek, & Goh Kiat Lian.

Jonny Hawkins was generous enough to allow me to reprint some of his cartoons in this book.

Here are my friends, colleagues, and mentors who received the first advanced review copies:

- Dr. David Austin: http://rt-blog.blogspot.com
- Charlie Dixon: www.recreationtherapy.com
- Heather Wyman: www.myspace.com/6degreesnj
- Kim Grandal: www.recreationtherapy.com
- Dr. Jeanine: www.simplydivinesolutions.com
- Logan Olson: www.loganmagazine.com
- Steve Manning: www.writeabooknow.com
- Dr. Joe Vitale: www.hypnoticwritingwizard.com

Several other people have mentored me in in-direct ways because I had read their books or taken their seminars.

These indirect mentors included:

- Dorothea Brande's (1981) *Becoming a Writer.*
- Mark Victor Hansen's (2007) *Mega Book Marketing University.*
- Joe Vitale's (2007) *Hypnotic Writing Wizard* book and software.
- Steven Pressifled's (2003) *The War of Art*: *Break Through the Blocks and Win Your Inner Creative Battles.*
- Steve Manning's *How to Write a Book Course.*

Group # 2: My family: I must acknowledge that I am very grateful to have been raised in a good, secure, and safe home with loving and caring parents. I have worked with children who have not had loving and caring homes. I am a very fortunate person and I realize this. I wouldn't be where I am today without my parents and two younger siblings. My parent's names are Danny and Teresa Pettry. My two younger sibling's names are Jimmy and Carrie Pettry. Our family also had a pet Chihuahua, Shadow, and several cats over the years, including: Sabo, Smokey, and currently, Onyx.

Group # 3: My patients: I've provided recreational therapy services for children and adolescents for over 6-years at an undisclosed location in one of the two Virginias. I am very fortunate to have the opportunity to serve these patients because this is meaningful work to me. I am very glad to provide them with opportunities for healing through the use of a variety of interventions. I feel satisfied at the end of the workday knowing that I am doing this type of work. I couldn't see myself doing anything else. I wish I could list a few names here, but I can't because of confidentiality reasons. I do want to say there have been a handful of children who have risen above their limitations and have became successful teens and productive members of society. I am always pleased to hear of their success stories.

Group # 4: Recreational Therapists: Many recreational therapists have inspired me and have been my teachers and mentors. Naturally, they've influenced my thinking. Here are some recreational therapists who've inspired me:

- Mark was the first recreational therapist who I'd met while doing volunteer work at HealthSouth Rehab of Huntington, WV in 1999.
- Marci Osborne was an intern at HealthSouth in 1999. She was the person who told me how I could become a recreational therapist, too.
- Dr. Sandra Parker was my undergraduate advisor at Marshall University (Huntington, West Virginia). She's still one of my personal mentors.
- Alane Thomas was my instructor at Marshall University and my internship supervisor at St. Mary's Medical Center of Huntington, WV.
- Charlie Dixon of Morgantown, WV operates the worldwide site, the Therapeutic Recreation Directory. I'm fortunate to say that he's one of my personal mentors, too.
- Dr. David Austin was my graduate advisor at Indiana University (Bloomington, Indiana).
- Dr. Bryan McCormick was one of my primary professors at Indiana University.
- Dr. Youngkhill Lee was one of my primary professors at Indiana University.
- Todd Wyrick helped me to obtain my first job as a recreational therapist.

Of course, many other recreational therapists have inspired me. It is always my pleasure to meet and network with other recreational therapists from around the world.

Table of Contents

Your Free Bonuses for Buying this Book!

You can download and print the following e-book:

Bonus # 1

Wisdom Revealed:
The Complimentary Journal on Becoming Great

It is available exclusively for you at this link online:

www.HiddenSecretWisdom.com/bonus

30+ More Bonuses

You're entitled to get 30+ more bonuses as my gift to you for buying this book. These gifts include e-books, articles on success and achievement, and more. They're written by some of the leading experts from around the world. This is a growing list. More articles will be added to help you on your quest to become the best.

These are available exclusively for you at this link online:

www.HiddenSecretWisdom.com/bonus

Introduction
-- Do You Make This Mistake In Life?

Learning all that you can is the secret to obtaining wisdom. You've got to have an open mind in order to learn. Be humble and realize that no one person knows it all. I've heard a wise saying: *search for people who are seeking wisdom and run from those who claim to know it all.*

A person who claims to know everything can't learn anything new. She (or he) won't open her mind to learn new things. As a result this person will prevent herself (or himself) from gaining any new wisdom. I'd argue that pride is a learning disability.

I'm humble. I realize that I don't know everything. I'd be willing to learn from you. I'm certain that you know things that I don't know. I'd be willing to take notes to learn from you, too.

My book, *Discover Hidden Secret Wisdom*, is about becoming great. Several people told me that they don't need a book on becoming great because they're already great. I agree with part of that statement. Yes, they're already great! However, the person who says that she (or he) doesn't need a book on becoming great is making a mistake in life. A person with this type of overconfident attitude can't learn anything new. This person feels that she (or he) already knows-it-all and as a result, can't learn. Don't make that mistake. Be humble and open to learning and growing. Give this book that you're holding in your hands a chance. Read the full book and share the hidden wisdom with other people.

Books can help you in your path of growth and development throughout life. **The key concept** of my book, *Discover Hidden Secret Wisdom,* is to encourage you to become great by being a lifelong reader. I want to you develop a passion for reading and learning.

Discover wisdom by reading. Books are filled with secrets, but you must be an active reader to reveal all the knowledge that is buried in books. Learn all the wisdom that you can through reading both fiction and non-fiction.

In this book, I'll review many books that I've read and reveal a few pearls of wisdom from many of my favorite books. Read some of the books that I suggest if you've not done so already. Discover everything that you can in life.

Here is a preview of what you'll discover in this book:

- **Chapter 1:** The first step that you must take

- **Chapter 2:** The most powerful tool for self-development and personal growth

- **Chapter 3:** The best way to gain wisdom on anything

- **Chapter 4:** The way successful people have already became great

- **Chapter 5**: The truth about teachers and why you need one

- **Chapter 6:** How movies can be used for personal development and self-improvement

- **Chapter 7:** How being happy can help you

- **Chapter 8:** How to become successful during your leisure

- **Chapter 9:** The best way to get a job or do anything

- **Chapter 10:** Why do-gooders are more likely to become successful

- **Chapter 11:** How a health and fitness program can help you to become successful and an easy/ free activity that you can do almost anywhere to get in-shape and stay-in-shape

- **Chapter 12:** How to use your potential energy and start becoming great with motivation techniques

Enjoy your exciting experience with this book.

Yours truly,

Danny Wayne Pettry, II, MS, CTRS
Recreational Therapist & Humanitarian

"Shhh ... don't spoil the ending for me."

© 2009 by Jonny Hawkins. Reprinted with permission. All rights reserved.

Chapter 1

Who Else Wants to Discover the First Step to Becoming Great?

"When you discover your mission, you will feel its demand. It will fill you with enthusiasm and a burning desire to get to work on it."

- W. Clement Stone

You're perfect

Snowflakes come in all different shapes and sizes. They're already perfect because they're created that way. They're big, small, puffy, flakey, icy, round, and many other forms. The list goes on. I've heard that Eskimos in the north have 1,000 names for white or snow.

There are no two people alike either. You're life is like a snowflake in that it will come to an end someday just like the snow will melt someday, too. Unlike a snowflake, you can improve while you're here. You have imagination, hopes, dreams, and abilities.

A snowflake is its best because it is the only snowflake like it in the world. There will not be a second one just like it. There will not be another person just like you in every detail. Twins have differences. A cloned you would not have your memories, experiences, and knowledge. Those are things that would still make you different. A cloned you would not be born with the talents you've developed. You're different and you're perfect. You're unique.

Be the best snowflake

Here is the secret: you've got to do your best in order to be the best. How else could you become the greatest in the world at anything? A person who sits at home watching re-runs on television will not become great at anything worthwhile. A person who does this may become great at television trivia. This person may be able to tell you what happened to

Rachel and Ross in *Friends* in episode four of season three. I don't know what happened to Rachel and Ross in that episode. You've got to actively improve some area of your life if you want to become the best. Sitting home watching television won't help you.

You're already the best you in the world because you're the only you. Are you doing your best? Are you getting better at anything daily? Can you say that you're better in one area of your life than you were this time last year? It could be in anything in the world? You could become better at playing guitar, writing, singing, golfing, money-management, quilting, swimming, or anything. Are you become better at anything?

Who are you?

This is a very important question to ask.

I attended a Clinical Supervision session in Kansas City at the American Therapeutic Recreation Association (ATRA) conference in 2004. We did a little warm-up exercise. Each person had one partner. My partner was Emily, a schoolteacher in North Carolina with a degree in recreational therapy from Indiana University.

I had to ask her one question: Who are you? She had to answer it in one-word answers. Her answers included: a woman, a daughter, a teacher, etc. You get the point. She continued to answer the question for five straight minutes. She asked me the same question for the next five-minutes. The goal was to get as many answers as possible in order to get to know the other person.

It is a great way to really think about who you are, too. You can do this little exercise alone or with another person. You could write your answers in a journal. Notice: this question is included in your complimentary journal. Download and print it at this link if you've not done so already:

www.HiddenSecretWisdom.com/bonus

Here are my answers: I'm a helper, a man, a brother, a son, an uncle, a cookie-lover, an artist, a writer, a reader, a doodler, a driver, an Indiana University graduate, a fan of the band, the Cure, a recreational therapist, and a blood-donor. This list goes on and on and so will yours. This is an excellent way for you to determine who you are. It is the first step towards becoming great. What good would it do you if you pursue something that isn't really you? Would you be satisfied trying to become great at something that isn't what you're all about?

What is your personality?

"Idealist/ healer" is my personality. It is one of 16 different types. Dr. Keirsey is the author of the (1998) book, *Please Understand Me II: Temperament, Character, Intelligence.* It's a book on personalities. There are four primary personalities according to Dr. Keirsey. These include: artists, idealist, guardians, and the rationalist. There are four sub-categories for each of the four temperaments. There are 16 total personalities within the four primary temperaments.

Keirsey's (1998) book has a really neat test in it. It's a great test because there isn't right or wrong answers. All answers are correct as long as you're honest.

You have one of these 16 personalities. Do you know what yours is? If not, take the quiz soon. I've taken the quiz twice. The first time was in 1999 during an introduction to college course and the second time was in 2006 at a leadership training course that I had taken. Both times I had the same personality, "a healer."

Keirsey.Com (Retrieved Jan. 2009) lists famous people who have each personality. Many great people who I admire also share the "Idealist" personality. These include: the late Princess Diana (Idealist/ healer), Dr. Carl Rogers (Idealist/ champion), Dr. Albert Schweitzer (Idealist/ healer), and Oprah Winfrey is an (Idealist/ teacher).

You could take the Keirsey Temperament test to determine your personality. You could go to Keirsey.Com online and discover famous people who share your personality. Knowing this information can help you on your path to becoming great.

Live your life the right way

What is the right way? I can't answer that for you. Only you know what is right for your life. You've got to make this choice for yourself because if you don't then somebody else will make it for you. If you don't know who you are then somebody else will attempt to make this choice for you. They'll say what you are and you could grow up to become just that. Psychologists call it a self-fulfilling prophecy, or the Pygmalion-effect, based on George Bernard Shaw's classic novel, *Pygmalion.* This is not good because they could determine that you're not good enough to do what you really want to do. You've got to decide what you want out of life. You must choose what you want to do in life and work towards that goal. That is the right way.

Nursing is what my mom and dad wanted me to major in at *Beckley College*, which is now known as *Mountain State University* in Beckley, West Virginia. They decided that this would be a good job for me. This was their choice. It wasn't mine. They told me that we would always need nurses. The world must have them. They said I could get a good job at a hospital and that I could make a decent living.

My father and grandfather were elementary school principals. It was the family business. As a child, I wanted to be a schoolteacher. I knew this by first grade. My parents got me a chalkboard for Christmas one year. I attempted to teach my two younger siblings, but they would have none of that. My brother Jimmy would say he hated school and had had enough of it already. I taught my stuffed animals, but that became boring. Finally, I found some willing students.

I taught my grandparents. They would let me play school when they babysat me. The healer personality has been in me since first grade. I know this because I didn't grade my grandparents on the math and spelling tests that I had given them. I graded them on their behavior. Were they motivated to take my tests? Were they being nice and kind that day? I graded them on their conduct and character.

Today, as an adult, I am a recreational therapist at a hospital located in one of the two Virginias. I am required to grade children. I do not like giving a grade. I am opposed to grading. I grade the children on social interaction. I've created a four-point scale based on: being polite, considerate, helpful, and working as a team-player. Basically, I list ways for each child to improve her (or his) social interaction skills based on their score. I share ways she (or he) could be more empathetic or considerate towards others during interventions that I provide. In general, children at my hospital are physically and verbally aggressive towards others. I suppose I am doing the job that I was always meant to do. I work as both a healer and a teacher as a recreational therapist.

Decide what you want to do with your life and do your very best at it. Most likely you do not want to be a recreational therapist like me. You've got to decide what it is that you want to do with your life and do it. This will make your life so much greater and enjoyable. Work at what you love to do.

What are your wildest dreams?

Wishes can come true. They happen to people all the time. Imagine if you had a magical lamp with a genie inside. This genie would have an exception to the wish rule. You'd get as many wishes as possible. Most people believe there are only three wishes or even one wish per genie. According to the original story about the genie in the lamp, a person had as many wishes as she (or he) wanted to make (Byrne, 2006). That life was full of possibilities. Maybe everyone had a magical lamp back then. Only a few people knew the secret that they could make as many wishes as they desired.

Have you ever heard of the saying, "be careful what you wish for because you just might get it?" This is very true. What you think about - you just might get. This is why some people have miracles in their lives. Books are filled with these stories. They're about people who survive things, achieve greatness, and do wonderful things. It happens and there is no reason that it shouldn't happen to you, too.

If you could have, do, or be anything: what would you have, do, or be? Write down your answers. Give 100 answers for each part: have, do, and be. These questions are also included in your complimentary journal.

It is possible for you to start doing some of these things on your list today. Your bigger wishes will take some time. You've probably heard that

Rome wasn't built in a day. A person doesn't become great at anything in one day.

What are your priorities?

Priorities are important things. They're ranked from most important to least important. There are no wrong priorities. It is your life and you decide what is most important. In a random order of areas, priorities could include: your religion, family, education, dating, leisure/ hobby, money, work/ career, or anything important to you. You've got to know what is most important to you. I'm not recommending that you should neglect all other areas in your life for one area. Here is an example: if your career is important, then naturally, you shouldn't neglect your family and friends or stop taking vacation and time to relax because you've identified your career as a priority. This would not be healthy. Balance is key. Priority lists are important so that you'll know what is important to you.

I knew a family who I felt had their priorities backwards. Maybe they had them right all along, but they were different priorities from mine. The parents didn't have jobs. They had a little house. What little money they had went into their magnificent boat. They practically lived on the boat all summer. I thought this was crazy. I'm older now and I realize their priorities were right for them. They were different from my priorities, but not better than the priorities I have for myself.

Dr. McCormick was one of my professors at Indiana University while I was working on my graduate degree in 2006. He taught students how to have more freedom during one course. His secret was for a person to do less. People who do more have more commitments and responsibilities. People who do less have more freedom. Here is a good example: A person who buys a lot of material things will have to work more to pay for it and to maintain its upkeep. They'll have to keep it safe, protected, clean, and in good condition. The family that I told you about earlier didn't have any debt. They lived within their means and they lived on their boat. Their priorities helped them to enjoy an easier, more relaxed life.

How do you spend your time?

Time is a passing moment. In a second it is gone forever. It'll never come back. Time is passing as I'm writing this chapter and as you're reading it. Passing time is the reason you've got to read this book fast. Don't put this book down yet. Keep reading. Determine the best way to use your time. Try to spend most of your time on your number one priority. Make sure your number one priority makes you happy.

You've got to determine how you use your time. What do you spend most of your time doing?

Here is a self-discovery exercise that will help you determine how you use your time. You don't have to do it now because this question is included in your complimentary journal that you can download online.

Instructions: Color each box in the grid a different color. Work could be red. Sleep could be black. Hygiene could be blue. Recreation and hobbies could be pink. Maintenance, yard work, housekeeping, and laundry could be orange. Watching television could be yellow. You can add colors for different things. These things could include: using the internet, spirituality/ church services, time with family, dating, playing a musical instrument, playing a sport, etc.

You may have 40 hours of blue for work or 20 hours of school, etc. What do you spend most of your time doing per week according to the colors? Put them in order from the top thing you do the most to the thing you do the least. Many people discover that they spend a large amount of time watching television.

Example of chart

Time	Su.	Mo.	Tu.	We.	Th.	Fi.	Sa.
6:30							
7:00							
7:30							
8:00							

Note: The full chart is in your complimentary journal that is available for you at this link: www.hiddensecretwisdom.com/bonus

Compare the list of your priorities to the list of how you spend your time. Ask yourself one major question: are you spending your time doing what is most important to you? If you are really interested in playing guitar, but you're always spending your spare time watching music videos on television then you could decide it is time to change. Spend more time doing what you think is most important. This will help you to start becoming great at what is important to you.

What would make your life better?

Time is limited here. Time on Earth is not forever. Imagine if you knew your life was about to end, what would you do to make what time you had left better? If you could do something to improve your life; what would it be? It could be anything in the world. Would you spend more time doing a certain something? You may want to spend more time painting, playing guitar, snowboarding, quilting, dating, fishing, golfing, or helping others? It could be anything. I've decided to use my time to write this book. It is my priority to help people like you.

Relationships: What would make your life better in this area? Could you have better relationships with your family or friends? Are you seeking to find a special relationship with a significant other? Do you need to improve the relationship with your current significant other? What do you want?

Skills are important. These are abilities to do things. In order to cook, you'd need cooking skills. In order to write, you'd need writing skills. Is there any skill that you would like to become better at? What skill would that be? Would you like to be better at computers, writing, or singing? What skills do you want to develop?   Answering these questions will help you to understand what would make your life better.

Decisions could be made for you by someone else if you're not clear about what you want. I told you earlier that my parents wanted me to major in nursing. I didn't want to be a nurse. It just wasn't right for me. I started attending college classes in 1998. I made the decision to change my course of study from nursing to recreational therapy because this is what I wanted to do with my life.

Choices were mine. I decided what classes I wanted to take. I decided what time to take them. I decided what hours to work at my part-time job. I decided what I wanted to major in while at college. It was my life. It was my choice and my responsibility. I would not allow other people to make these choices for me. They can't make these choices for you, unless you allow them. Parents, friends, co-workers, and other people could decide who you'll date and who you'll marry. They could decide where you'll work and what job you'll have and the clothes you wear and every thing about your life. That is a total lack of freedom and choice. I believe in autonomy (You having the freedom and independence to choose what is best for you). You get to decide what you want to be. It's your life and your choice.

What is your perfect day?

Perfect days can be very different from one another. No two perfect days are alike. You could have many perfect days. I would get extremely bored having one perfect day which I lived over and over again. Christmas or other holidays may seem like perfect days, but I imagine that if you had Christmas or the 4th of July every day of the year then you'd start to hate it. You can have many different perfect days. What is your perfect work day? What is your perfect vacation day? What is your perfect day with your family?

Where would you like to go in life?

Dr. Seuss has written a wonderful little book called, *Oh, the Places You'll Go*. It is often given to graduates of kindergarten, high school, and college. I like how it is given to all ages. I have a copy of this book. I often read it to the children who I provide services for during therapeutic story time. I ask them where they'd like to go in life. The book is motivational and inspirational. Near the end of the book, it reads:

And will you succeed?
Yes! You will, indeed!
(98 and 3/4 percent guaranteed.)

- Dr. Seuss (1990)

Oh, how marvelous are the words of Dr. Seuss! His words could make a person feel great.

Another great book that you may want to consider is *1,000 Places to See Before You Die: A Traveler's Life List* by Patricia Schultz. Write down a list of 100 places you'd like to see before you die. This is a very fun project.

I have my own personal list. I want to see the holocaust museum in Washington D.C., the Mall of America in Minnesota, the president Truman Library in Missouri. Create a list of 100 places you want to see.

The Hidden Secret Revealed in Chapter 1:

Know who you are and what you want.

*** Upcoming Attraction ***

Writing can help you in the process of self-discovery. Continue to the next chapter to discover how keeping a journal can help you to become great.

Chapter 1 References

About 4 Temperaments (n.d.) Retrieved online January 2009, from: http://keirsey.com/handler.aspx?s=keirsey&f=fourtemps&tab=3&c=healer

Bryne, R. (2006). *The Secret*. New York,NY: Atria Books/Beyond Words.

Hutchins, D., Cooke, C., & Negley, S. (2004, Sept. 30). *Clinical supervision*. Presented at the American Therapeutic Recreation Association annual conference in Kansas City, Missouri: ATRA

Keirsey, D. (1998). *Please Understand Me II: Temperament, Character, and Intelligence*. Del Mar, California: Prometheus Nemesis Book Company.

Margetta, D. & Blackman, S. (2006, March 17). *Leadership development*. Presented at the American therapeutic Recreation Association mid-year conference in Washington, D.C.

McCormick, B. (Professor). (2006). Lecture on leisure and freedom. Presented at Indiana University, Bloomington, IN.

Schultz, P. (2003). *1,000 Places to See Before You Die: A Traveler's Life List*. Chicago: Workman Publishing Company.

Seuss, D. (1990). *Oh, the Places You'll Go!*. Random House Children's Books.

Chapter 2

This is the Most Powerful Tool Used for Self-Development and Personal Growth

"Ideas are elusive, slippery things. Best to keep a pad of paper and a pencil at your bedside, so you can grab them during the night before they get away."

- Earl Nightingale

Use a journal

Tools are things that a person uses in order to accomplish something. A journal is a wonderful tool that many of the greatest people use. Jack Canfield, co-creator of *Chicken Soup* book series, and motivational speaker Jim Rohn both use journals. Presidents use them. Artists use them. Song writers and musicians use them.

I work at a hospital. All the children are required to keep a journal. They're called "thought logs" at my hospital. It kind of reminds me of a captain's log.

A journal is more than just a record of what happened in your day. Here is a list of things this tool can help you do:

- Write a record of personal goals
- Write a collection of good ideas
- Jot down things so you'll remember them
- Keep a record of wisdom that you've learned from reading books
- Track your progress
- Keep important lists and notes
- Record inspirational quotes
- Express emotions and feelings

If you've not done so already, download and print your complimentary journal at this link:

www.hiddensecretwisdom.com/bonus

What does a person need to start?

Journals that are suitable for you are the best. You've got to decide what kind you want. It can have lines or blank pages. It could be a dollar store notebook, a yellow legal pad, or expensive leather bound book. I like to use a spiral bound hardcover journal myself because they are easy to fold. Keep in mind, a journal containing acid free paper will preserve your writings for future generations.

Something to write with is needed. I've found one technique that encourages children to write. I allow them to write with anything they want. They can use a pencil, a colored ink-pen, or a crayon. I provide a selection of colored ink pens which are their favorites. There are also acid free ink pens to preserve writings for longer periods of time.

Timers can be an important tool for using a journal. I learned this technique from Roberta Allen's (2002) book, *The Playful Way to Serious Writing*. She suggested that a timer motives people to write. It works. I've written every section of this whole book in five-minute increments. Over time, these five-minute increments have added up to the 12 chapter book that you're holding in your hands now.

You only need these things:

- A journal
- Something to write with
- A timer (optional, but helpful).

You need time to write. This could be the first five minutes of the day or the last five minutes. It could be five during your lunch break or while waiting at a doctor's office. There are plenty of five minute breaks during the day where you're just waiting that you could use productively for journaling.

You could use a journal

Anyone can use a journal. It doesn't matter if you're a young person or a person who is elder. You could have special needs or a small vocabulary and you could still do it. Anyone can do it.

I've provided journaling as a treatment tool for children. Often times, male students will say, "guys don't keep a journal." They think it is an activity for women. Here is my favorite motivator: Ronald Reagan kept a journal. It has been said that he kept one of the most detailed diaries among all U.S. Presidents while in office. He was a writer. He had written his own speeches before getting elected. He had also written poetry, short-stories, and stories about sports throughout his life. Ronald Reagan was a male, so guys can keep a journal, too.

Starting a journal could be a powerful tool for self-development and personal growth. If a person like Ronald Reagan can use a journal his whole life then so can you.

How I use a journal

First, I'll just number the odd pages because they are on the right side, which is usually the first page a person reads. I've heard that magazines even charge more for advertisements on right pages (odd numbered pages) because a person sees these pages more often when just flipping through a magazine opposed to the even pages (on the left side).

Second, I create a "table of contents" in the front of the journal. It includes the sections I want in my journal. Sections in my personal journal include: goals, ideas and wisdom from books I've read, ideas from training sessions, dreams I had last night, ideas for writing, and good deeds to do. Then I section them off. Section one could be for pages one to 15 and section two will be for pages 16 to 30. You get to select which pages you want.

Motivational speaker, Jim Rohn (1993) has a neat little C.D. called, *How to use a Journal.* It is about 45-minutes long. I've learned some excellent techniques from him. He suggests keeping an index. This is so you'll be able to find things in your journal. Your index could have titles like: dreams, quotes, lessons, creative ideas, etc. In example, good quotes could be found on pages: 2, 10, and 25. Jim Rohn also says that you should review your journal often.

Don't worry about mistakes. Sometimes the children who I provide services will say, "I messed up," and they'll tear a page out. I don't believe in doing that. The page could have information that you may find useful later. Keep all pages in there.

Don't worry about spelling. Make sure that you can read it. Use abbreviations if you want. It is your journal. Most people would not be able to read mine because I've created my own short hand technique of abbreviations and symbols.

An artist's journal

Earl Nightingale had recorded the first inspirational talk that sold one-million copies, called, *The Strangest Secret in the World*. Nightingale had also written a short story called "Sparky" that is featured in Jack Canfield, Mark Victor Hansen, and Kimberly Kirberger (2003) book, *Chicken Soup for the Teenage Soul: 101 Stories of Life, Love and Learning*.

This story was about a boy who was a loser. He doesn't do anything well. He did enjoy art and felt good at it. He didn't write in a journal, but he had written his life story in cartoons through the use of art in a journal. He found this to be his way of expression. He felt so confident about his art that he took it to *Disney*. But, *Disney* said his art was no good. This was what he loved to do. He continued doing what he loved and he published his life story. Who was Sparky? You may know him as the creator of *Peanuts*. He was Charles Shultz. The character Charlie Brown was based on his own life. Drawing can be used as an alternative if you don't like to write.

A journal can also be used as a healing tool. A person can achieve more greatness once they are in the process of healing and getting better. You may not need therapy, but a journal can still be a powerful self-development tool.

Solving problems through journaling

The Committee for Children (1998) has an excellent format for solving problems. It's presented in their *Second Step* social skills curriculum for children. Here is an overview of how you can solve a problem, based on the *Second Step* Program:

- Write down the problem. Define the problem as clearly as possible.

- Write down some solutions, no matter how wild they may seem. Ask yourself: is this a solution that is safe and fair? Consider how other people will feel if you were to choose a solution.

- Ask yourself: will this solution work? If yes, then use it. If not, repeat the process and find a new solution. It is that easy.

What if you select a solution that does not work? Then you've had a learning experience. That is the beauty of life lessons. You'll continue to get the same lesson over and over again until you learn it. Sometimes, kids will ask me for a solution. I can't always give them one. An example is when a child asked me once, should I choose to live with my mother or my father? This child had the choice to choose. I couldn't make that choice for her.

Express emotions through journaling

Journals can be used to express emotions, too. You can write a four-step process, which includes: event, thoughts, feelings, and solutions.

First, you write an event that has happened in your life. It can be a positive event or it can be a negative event. Then you describe it in details. After that you write your main feelings about the event. You could have more than one feeling. If a friend moves, you could feel sad about it and you could be glad that they are moving on to something better. This is especially true when high school friends separate and go to different colleges.

Benefits for expressing emotions

There are many benefits for expressing emotions. James Pennebaker has presented a major portion of the research in his (1997) book, *Opening Up: The Healing Power of Expressing Emotions.* Scientific studies have proven that people who have experienced trauma fare better if they keep a journal about thoughts and feelings, compared to those who do not keep one. Research has also pointed out that college kids who keep a journal about daily personal feelings are less likely to see the campus physician than those who do not keep a journal.

Here are two examples of how writing a journal and expressing emotions have helped people around the world:

- **Example 1: Teacher, Erin Gruewell's students.** (Source: Gruewell's & the freedom writer's, 2006).

Erin Gruewell was a new teacher at Woodrow Wilson High School of Long Beach, California. She got the worst students because she was the "new" teacher. The teachers with more seniority would get the classes full of children who were "well-behaved." Children in her class were into gangs. They had race wars. Kids were getting shot and killed over their skin color. It was a war.

Gruewell taught English to these kids, but she realized quickly that they needed more than English. She went the extra mile for these teens in her class. She wanted to help them to become better people and to succeed in life. Teaching English alone would not do it. She had to do more to reach out to these troubled teens. She had the teens to read stories about the holocaust. They read *Anne Frank's Diary* and many other books about people who have suffered. The students could identify with the characters in the books and apply situations to their own lives.

The teens in Gruewell's class had to keep their own diary. They filled them up with horrific stories about their own personal tragedies. Today, this book is published. It is called, *The Freedom Writers Diary: How a Teacher and 150 Teens Used Writing to Change Themselves and the World Around Them.* Here is a brief quote from the book that reveals that expressing thoughts and feelings is beneficial:

> "I was getting everything off my chest and it felt damn good. I continued to tell the class that my father had molested my sister and how angry I was that my mother didn't do anything when she found out about it."
>
> Diary Entry # 56, *Freedom Writer's Diary* (2006).
>
> Her comment demonstrates the benefit for expressing emotions as evidenced by her stating that it: **"felt good."**

- **Example 2: Zlata Filipović** (Source: Filipović, 1994).

Zlata Filipović is one of my heroes. Terrible things happened in Sarajevo in 1991 and Zlata had written about the happenings. Her diary told a story about her life during a time when a civil war had broken out in her country. Zlata was a 12-year-old girl living in the country at this time. Until then, her life had been fairly normal. She went to school, spent time with friends, and enjoyed life.

She lost the opportunity to do all the wonderful, fun things in life when the war began. She had to move into her basement to live with her family. She wasn't able to be near a window or she could be shot. She couldn't go to school because of shootings and bombs. She couldn't do many things. Her family lived without heat during the winter and without running water. Things were terrible for her. Zlata experienced horrors and tragedies that I'll never know personally beyond reading her book, titled, *Zlata's Dairy*. Many of her friends died as the result of the war.

She kept a dairy during the full time the war was happening. Where is she today? Her diary was published. It gave her the opportunity to get out of the country. She went to Oxford in Ireland and graduated with a B.A. in human science. She works at promoting human rights worldwide, which I think is great. I personally want to speak to her about how her journal has been an inspiration in my life.

Zlata used a dairy to help her cope with tragedies in her life. These tragedies are far worse than what most of us have seen or experienced. If keeping a journal worked for Zlata then it can work for you, too.

Writing was her escape during the war that helped keep her sane. Zlata suggested that writing could be one of the "best vehicles" for Mrs. Gruewell's students to "escape the horrific enviorments and personal demons according to a comment she made that is listed in the (1999) book, *Freedom Writer's Diary.*

The Hidden Secret Revealed in Chapter 2:

Use a success journal to become great.

*** Upcoming Attraction ***

Journaling is most often best combined with reading. Erin Gruewell (2006) had her students read and keep a journal. Please continue to the next chapter to learn how reading books could make you successful.

Chapter 2 References

Allen, R. (2002). *The Playful Way to Serious Writing*. New York: Mariner Books.

Committee for Children. (1998). Second Step violence prevention curriculum. Committee for Children.

Filipovic. (1994). *Zlatas Diary A Childs Life In Sarajevo*. New York: Scholastic.

Gruwell, E., & Writers, T. F. (2006). *The Freedom Writers Diary: Movie-Tie-In: How a Teacher and 150 Teens Used Writing to Change Themselves and the World Around Them*. New York City: Broadway.

Nightingale, E. (1997). Sparky. In J. Canfield, M. Hansen, &K. Kirberger's *Chicken soup for the teenage soul: 101 stories of love, life, and learning*. Deerfield Beach, FL: Health Communications, Inc.

Pennebaker, J. W. (1997). *Opening Up: The Healing Power of Expressing Emotions*. New York: The Guilford Press.

Rohn, J. (1993). *How to use a journal*. [audio recording cassette]. Dallas, TX: Jim Rohn International.

Chapter 3

At Last! Here's How to Discover Hidden Secret Wisdom on Becoming Great

"There is more treasure in books than in all the pirates' loot on Treasure Island… and best of all, you can enjoy these riches every day of your life."

- Walt Disney

What wisdom do you want revealed?

Love and <u>passion</u> are strong emotions. What do you love the most? What are you most passionate about? This could be anything in the world. You've got to decide what it is. If you've read chapter one on self-discovery, then you could already know what you want to do with your life. You know what you love. Here is a self-awareness question: If you could go to a great library and study or read about anything in the world, what would you go to learn about? It could be about art, poetry, playing the guitar, learning how to cook, how to build a house, or anything. This great library would have every book, magazine, and important document in the world. You probably drive by a library every so often, maybe even daily. Did you realize you're driving right by a place with treasure maps? These are books that outline the steps to become great at what you want to be. You could go and read about anything in the world.

Many people say they hate books and that they don't read them. I believe they just haven't found the right book yet. Once they find that right book then they'll change their attitude. It'll be a book that she (or he) simply can't put down. It'll be a real page-turner.

> Anything in the world can be found in books.

> Literacy is the # 1 skill needed for becoming great.

What is hidden wisdom?

Posey Boyd Pettry was my grandfather. He passed away before I was born. I never had the opportunity to meet this biological grandfather. I know very little about him. He was an elementary school principal like my father, Danny Pettry (senior).

Posey had taken wisdom and knowledge to the grave with him when he passed away. He had taken every single thing he had ever learned with him when he died. His knowledge, wisdom, and life experiences are gone for good.

I wasn't born with any of it. The knowledge and wisdom wasn't passed down to me. This type of information is not passed down to anyone. There is not a single human being who is born with all the knowledge of their parents, grand-parents, or their great-great-grandparents. Ancestors who lived thousands of years ago have more knowledge than a new born baby in today's world of technology.

Every human being must start the learning process on her (or his) own. They must learn the alphabet, learn how to count, learn how to talk, learn how to walk, and do everything for the first time. It would be easier if humans were born with wisdom, knowledge, and a few skills. However, we must learn on our own.

Books contain hidden secret wisdom from generations from a long time ago. My grandfather, Posey, could have written a book about his life experiences. He could have outlined sound advice for his kids and grand kids and even his great-grand kids. That would have been excellent. I would love to have read a book from him.

Books are the best way for learning how to become great. You could learn a lot of wisdom from a dead person. In fact, I've read several books by people who've been dead for over 70-years. James Allen, author of *As a Man Thinketh* passed away in 1912. Russell Conwell, author of *Acres of Diamonds* passed away in 1925. *Advantages of Poverty* was written by millionaire philanthropist, Andrew Carnegie who passed away in 1919. Some of their advice and wisdom is absolutely astonishing. I would have never discovered this information without reading their books. Books can help reveal secret wisdom.

You learned in the previous chapter that you must keep a journal. Write notes in your journal from the books you read. You may discover something awesome in a book, but may never find it again. I always jot down meaningful quotes in my journal. I include the name of the author, the title of the book, the quotes page number, and the publisher. That way I know where I found it. Recently I read something fascinating and I didn't document it in my journal. I wanted to share the story of a girl who was told she'd never be a dancer and to quit because she had a learning disorder. Here is the fun part. This girl with the (disorder) grew up and started a well-known famous dance school. I may never find who this dancer was, but I had read about her in a book once. Write what you learn from books in your journal, so you'll be able to store your newfound wisdom.

How did Truman become great?

Harry S. Truman is my all-time favorite U.S. President. Many scholars argue that Truman was one of greatest of all U.S. Presidents in history.

I discovered how to become great while reading an old, musty, and out-of-print book, called, *President from Missouri: Harry S. Truman.* It was a great biography of the 33rd president by Ralph C. Martin (1964). It shared the whole life of Truman, from a farmer in a small town until he became President of the U.S.

How did Truman become great? What was his secret? Martin revealed that Truman loved reading, especially about his favorite heroes. Here is an amazing fact: Truman read every single book from his home town, Independence, Missouri public library. That is an accomplishment. His mother had given him a gift of books on courage that featured biographies on many great people. Truman read them and re-read them.

He studied people who were great. This strongly influenced him. He realized that all great people have common characteristics. Some of my favorite characteristics about Truman were that he was big on: honesty, integrity, and accountability. He started a program when he was a Senator from Missouri during WWII that investigated fraudulent and wasteful spending of government money. Many companies in America were billing the government a lot of money for services, but they were not producing the best products. It is like the old joke that they're selling hammers to the U.S. government for a $100. Truman looked into doing what was right and did it and saved the government a lot of money.

Don't listen to me

Here is my disclaimer notice. You may laugh aloud, but I didn't read a full book until I was 18-years-old. I knew how to read. I just didn't want to read books. As a result, I missed out on some of the greatest treasured classics like: Mary Shelley's *Frankenstein*, Lewis Carroll's *Alice in Wonderland*, George Bernard Shaw's *Pygmalion*, Frances Burnett's *A Little Princess*, Roald Dahl's *Matilda*, and Penelope Farmer's *Charlotte Sometimes*. Please note I have gone back and read all these classics and others that I had missed out on as a child.

One of my most embarrassing moments was during my Jr. High School years. My cousin, Tracy was babysitting me and my two younger siblings: Jimmy and Carrie. Tracy found a neat, well-written book report and a half written book report that was obviously written in a child's handwriting. My cousin put two and two together. She laughed and said, "Your mom writes your book reports." She had me. It was true. My loving and caring mother had great intentions. She wanted to help me and didn't want me to fail.

My mother has had a strong impact on my reading in an indirect way. She is a book-lover who has modeled the reading habit. She's read every book by some authors, including: Stephen King (horror), Nicholas Sparks (romance), and Dean Koontz (mystery). I love to hear when my mother gets a new book because I know I'll get to read it next.

I developed the reading habit when I read my first book as a senior in high school. I found a copy of Dale Carnegie's *How to Win Friends and Influence People* on a table at the school library. I was mesmerized by the title.

A beautiful girl named Bethany was the library assistant. Bethany had been my 9th-Grade Junior High School prom date. Besides that one dance, I hadn't talked much to Bethany. I was certainly too embarrassed to have her check the book out for me on winning friends, so I snuck it in my book-bag. Don't worry, I secretly returned it to the library several days later and I do the right thing when renting books from a library today. I recommend that you do the right thing when checking out books, too. I went and bought my own copy of *How to Win Friends and Influence People*, which I still own today. This book is one of my treasured classics. It has dog-eared pages with highlighted words and notes scribbled in the margins. All people should read this book. Carnegie's book has had a deep impact on my life. It was the book that taught me people skills and it got me addicted to reading.

Since reading my first book, I've read hundreds of self-improvement books on motivation, success, and achievement over the last decade. My personal library has over 500 books. I keep the self-improvement books and give away most novels after reading them. Self-improvement books put me in a hypnotic state of being. I awake from a reading spell ready to succeed.

Still, I don't know it all. That said; please know that I strongly advise you to read inspirational and motivational books and to learn all that you can. Don't believe everything you read in a book just because it is in a book. In fact, <u>Don't Believe Anything I've Written in This Book.</u> Anyone can write a book and have it published. Think about what you read carefully and decide for yourself if it is good material.

Bibliotherapy

Healing through the use of books is one of the techniques that recreational therapists use for treating patients. The basic concept is that reading is good-experience that can bring about healing outcomes and health promotion.

A person who is depressed could read a book about another person who is depressed or have experienced similar situations. This would be more powerful if the character in the story solved some problem. Naturally, one would not recommend that a depressed person read a book where the character commits suicide. Common sense is advised. A person who is depressed could benefit from reading, *A Joke a Day Keeps the Doctor Away* by Bob Phillips and Jonny Hawkins, or *Happy for No Reason: 7 Steps to Becoming Happy from the Inside Out* by Marci Shimoff (with Carol Kline).

As you already know, I provide recreational therapy services for children. I have therapeutic story sessions with these kids every so often. All of the younger children have been abused in some way. There is a great book for these children that help them in the process of opening up. It is called, *No More Secrets for Me* by Oralee Wachter (1986). It has four short stories, in which children experienced uncomfortable things and it teaches the children to "Tell - Tell - Tell." If an adult does not believe them, they must continue telling until someone does. It is a great way to educate children.

Stories are a great way to teach and heal. Bibliotherapy can use any books. A person could read fiction, non-fiction, self-help books or even pamphlets and handouts regarding an issue.

Read self-improvement books

Advancement requires you to get better at things. Reading a self-improvement book could give you the leading edge. You may have read about bibliothearpy above and could be thinking that you don't need therapy. That is okay, too.

You could still discover a lot of great things from books. Think about people who are the best at what you want to be great at doing. Most likely they've written books or somebody has written a book for them on their techniques. This is a top secret key to success.

You'll get the winner's edge by reading it. You'll have knowledge, skills, and awareness that other people may not know. Read 100 books on a given topic. You'll be more knowledgeable for a job interview and what to do when on the job. This will especially give you advancement over the person who has not read any of those 100 books.

People are not born naturally talented. I told you earlier, I was not born with any wisdom from my great-grand parents or anyone before that. I had to learn everything on my own. I've came a long way because I couldn't even write my own name the day I was born. I had to develop this skill.

I studied to become a great writer. I am a much better writer compared to the skills I had five-years ago, ten years ago, or even 25 years ago. I did it by reading and writing. One book that helped me the most was Joe Vitale's (2006) *Hypnotic Writing: How to Seduce and Persuade Customers with Only Your Words*. I've got a collection of books on writing techniques because I knew I wanted to be a great writer (or at least the best that I could be).

You on the other hand will need to get self-improvement and how-to books in the area that you want to be great at. It could be on gardening, swimming, being a better teacher, nurse, skateboarder, or golfer. You need to get these books. Subscribe to magazines in the area of your interest because they'll recommend books. Consider getting books on C.D. so you can listen to them in your car or commute to and from work or school.

Fiction books and non-fiction books are good for reading. Fiction could have stories in which the person achieves success in some uncanny, new way. Non-fiction books spell out exactly what you must do. Consider reading biography and autobiography. Create a list of five people who are great in the area that you want to be great at. If you want to be a great musician then read the biographies about your five favorite musicians. You could find these to be valuable. They may have hidden wisdom on how to become great and successful. You've got to read the book to uncover the secrets.

How to tell if a book is good or not

I've came across a few unpleasant books. I hope you don't think this is one of them. Please laugh aloud about that comment. It was meant to add some humor. I love reading and I seek out the best books.

Here are a few of my secrets that you can use to determine if a book is good or not before you buy it and read it.

Turn on your computer. Go online to *Amazon.com* and look at its average stars on the rating scale. (Notice: if you don't have a computer or internet access, the local library has computers you can use for free). *Amazon* has a "5" star rating scale. People can vote on the book. If it has a "5" star average then I may consider it. If only one person voted on it then I realize that an average of "5" may not be reliable. If 1,000 people have voted on it and it has an average of "4" stars, then I trust that it is a good book. *Amazon.com* allows readers to post their comments. It will show the best comments as well as the worst.

Google search "the name of the book" and the word "review." *Google* will give you a list of online book reviews that you can read. Many of these book reviews are published free in blogs. Read a couple of them before you decide to buy. If they are all negative then you might want to consider finding another book.

Ask friends, co-workers, and family members if they've read the book. They could give good advice. Therapists who I work with often email me with the title of a new book when it is out because we often read similar books on becoming better therapists.

Where is the goldmine?

Here is the information you've been waiting for. Goldmines are places where gold is buried and hidden. Gold is valuable. It's worth a lot. Your public library is a FREE goldmine and it contains the treasure maps to success. There is a book about anything you've dreamed about doing. There are books written by experts on getting anything you want to have, do, or be. Someone has already done it and they've outlined their steps to success. They show you how to get the gold (something you're seeking). Go sign-up for a library card today and rent at least one book in an area that you want to become greater at.

My favorite motivational speaker, Jim Rohn had said the following according to his (2001) booklet, called, *Treasury of Quotes:*

"Everything you need for a better future and success has already been written. And guess what? It's all available. All you have to do is go to the library.

> But, guess what? Only 3% of people in America have a library card. Wow, they must be expensive! No, they're free."

The Hidden Secret Revealed in Chapter 3:

Read a book a week, at least.

*** Upcoming Attraction ***

Studying and reading about great people worked for Harry Truman. It could be an excellent way for you to become great. Continue on to the next chapter to learn more hidden secret wisdom.

Chapter 3 References

Martin, R. G. (1964). *President from Missouri: Harry S. Truman.* Julian Messner, First Edition.

Rohn, J. (2001). *Treasury of quotes.* Dallas, TX: Jim Rohn International.

Vitale, J. (2006). *Hypnotic Writing: How to Seduce and Persuade Customers with Only Your Words.* New York, NY: Wiley.

Wachter, O. (1986). *No More Secrets For Me: Read Together Stories To Help Your Child Avoid Sexual Abuse.* London: Penguin Books.

"Your quest for inner peace begins by
cuddling up with a good book."

© 2008 Jonny Hawkins

© 2009 by Jonny Hawkins. Reprinted with permission.
All rights reserved.

Chapter 4

Discover What Successful People Already Know About Being Great

"Formal education will make you a living. Self-education will make you a fortune."

- Jim Rohn

Study successful people

Learn the secrets from the greatest people in the world. It'll help you in your process towards becoming great. People who are great at doing something already know how to do it the best way possible. You need to seek them out and learn all that you can.

Learning information on your own could take a long time. Why take the long, hard path in trying to learn how to do something? Trial and error takes time. Save time by learning from someone who has already achieved success. Here is a good example. A person who lives next door has the telephone number for a service that you need. It is an excellent service, but it isn't listed in the phone book. Which would be easier? Answer one: Try your best to find the number on your own independently. Answer two: Just go ask your next door neighbor because you know that person has the number. It could take hours, days, weeks, or even years for you to find it on your own. It would only take a second to learn the number by asking your neighbor.

Sadly, many people do this with big things they want to achieve. They don't go ask someone for many reasons. It could be fear, embarrassment, or any other reason. The wise thing for you to do is to go and seek out someone who is great because they have secret knowledge on how they became great.

Here is another example. Say a person wants to be a great guitar player. She could struggle to learn on her own. She buys a guitar and plays everyday, but unfortunately she does not know how to use it. As you can imagine, her music sounds not-so-wonderful. Wouldn't it be better for her to go to someone who is a great player and ask for lessons? She could ask a friend who plays or sign-up for lessons at the guitar shop. It is that easy. Go seek out someone who is great.

People who have achieved success are discussed in this chapter. I'm going to share brief reviews of their books to reveal hidden, secret wisdom. I think literacy is the number one skill needed to become great and successful. I hope you'll finish this chapter with a burning desire to read more books.

Dream of greatness

Happiness is the American dream or at least the pursuit of it. People want to obtain happiness and success. The secrets to how many great Americans achieve success is hidden in a little book called *The Daily Dose of the American Dream* by Alan C. Elliott (1998). It contains stories of *success, triumph, and inspiration.* Elliott's book includes 366 short and simple pages. There is one page for each day of the year. Get it and use your journal as you read. Jot down notes from each lesson and how you could use the information for your own American Dream.

Great Americans are discussed in Elliott's (1998) book. You'll learn how people like Sam

Walton (creator of *Wal-Mart*); Dave Thomas (creator of *Wendy's)*; Calvin Klein, Walt Disney, Bill Gates, Michael Jordon, and Harry Truman became great. You'll discover hidden wisdom in this book that you could use to become great. Reading about these Americans could inspire you, too.

Great people have some common characteristics. These include simple things like persistence, positive attitude, and treating other people nicely. All great people persist and keep at whatever it is that they want to become great at doing. Giving up is not an option. They'll prevail or die trying. Patrick Henry was one of the great revolutionists during the American Revolution. He knew that he wanted freedom and liberty. Henry is most known for his speech, "Give Me Liberty or Give Me Death." The point that I'm making is to go for what you want. Keep at it until the end.

A gift for Christmas

Christmastime was just around the corner in 1999. I had seen a book at *Wal-Mart* with an interesting title called *The 7 Habits of Highly Effective Teens* by Sean Covey (1998). I knew I wanted to read this book because it had secrets on becoming a successful teen. My mother and father had asked me keep an eye out for things that I might want to get for Christmas. I told them that I was 100% sure that I wanted this book. My mother gave a little laugh at first because of the title. She is an avid reader who prefers fiction. She has never been known to read a self-improvement book based on my memories. She said, I'd be turning 20 in March and would no longer be a teenager. I had about three months to read this book and she didn't think I should get it. I kind of dropped the idea of getting it for Christmas at that moment.

Surprise, I got a new book for Christmas. It was like the *Christmas Story* where Ralphie gets his gun. You always remember the words, "you'll shoot your eye out," if you've seen the *Christmas Story.* I can almost hear my mother saying something similar: "Self-improvement books never work." My parents loved me and they gave me *The 7 Habits of Highly Effective Teens* by Sean Covey. It was amazing. I've read it many times. I discovered that Sean had written this book based on his father's bestselling book, called, *The 7 Habits of Highly Effective People.* I've not read his father's book yet, so I can't review it. I think all teens should read Sean Covey's book. The knowledge they learn will help them throughout their transition from the teens to young adulthood. Young adults could benefit from reading this book, also. It may help them adjust to adulthood.

Learn the habits

A review of Sean Covey's (1998) *The 7 Habits for Highly Effective Teens.* Published by Fireside.

"A stitch in time saves nine" is an old saying that my grandmother, Donna Keesee, often said. It is a pro-active approach. It means that you act before a big problem occurs because a big problem is a lot harder to fix. It is the opposite of re-action where a person re-acts to big problems after they've taken place. It is best to be prepared. My professor in graduate school, Dr. Bryan McCormick (2006) argued that "chance favored the prepared." People who are prepared will be luckier. Sean Covey (1998) discusses being pro-active.

Covey's (1998) book is filled with many good ideas. You'll learn more than just seven good habits. Here is a basic overview of the Covey's next six habits beyond being pro-active:

- Have a vision. Know what you want to do in your life. Focus on it.

- Put your priorities in order and do the most important thing first.

- Do well. Be a person who makes the world a better place.

- Find solutions that work for everyone.

- Be empathetic and understanding. Try to listen and understand others.

- Take time for rest and relaxation. As a recreational therapist, I can say this is very important. Covey (1998) uses the metaphor of a saw that never gets re-sharpened. A dull saw is not effective. The saw needs a break from sawing to re-sharpen. You need to re-create yourself through recreation. Notice the hyphenation: [re-creation] Do activities that are relaxing and enjoying. Take time to rejuvenate yourself. You've probably heard the old motto, "all work and no play make Jack a dull boy." Take some time for yourself, too. You'll get a full chapter on leisure and recreation in an upcoming chapter. Keep reading.

Read *The Success Principles*

A review of Jack Canfield with Janet Switzer's (2005) *The Success Principles: How to Get from Where You Are to Where You Want to Be.* Published by: Collins Living

Jack Canfield is the co-creator of the bestselling *Chicken Soup* book series. He is in the book of world records for having seven books on the *New York Times Best Seller* list at the same time.

A boy who I'll call "Johnny" was a teen at the hospital where I work. He said he wanted to write a book, but said he couldn't get published because he is from West Virginia. He said that hurt him. I told him that the best-selling author, Jack Canfield was raised in little Wheeling, West Virginia. If he can do it and he was from West Virginia then you could do it. The book you're holding in your hands right now is written by a West Virginian. I'm from the small town of Beckley, West Virginia. I enjoy writing and having a book published was my goal.

The Success Principles by Jack Canfield (2005) is one of my favorite all-time books. It includes 64 principles that a person needs to use in order to be successful. I absolutely love the book. I've got his success principles recording on C.D. and DVD as well. You may want to use Canfield's book, CD, and DVD as motivational tools. You may want to find someone who you admire and use their words to inspire you.

I first discovered Canfield's book in 2006. I hadn't even realized that the book had been out since 2005. I immediately went to the local public library to rent a copy of this book.

How Canfield's book helped me

Salt Lake City, Utah was hosting the annual conference for recreational therapists during the summer of 2006. It was presented by the American Therapeutic Recreation Association. I was reading Canfield's book while many recreational therapists from across the United States and from around the world were gathering at this conference. I wanted to attend this conference, but unable to do so because of work obligations. I don't want to be an average, mediocre therapist who just goes to work and then comes home. I want to be the greatest recreational therapist in the world or at least the best that I can be. I knew that if I were at that conference then I could surround myself with the greatest recreational therapists. I could learn from the speakers and meet and network with other recreational therapists.

I called the association's office while recreational therapists were in Utah for the conference. I asked the secretary when the next conference was. She informed me that the mid-year conference for recreational therapists would be in March 2007 in Washington, D.C.

Jack Canfield helped me to attend the mid-year conference in March 2007. One of the success principles was to ask for what you want. His book inspired me to call the association and get details on the next conference and print out the cost.

Next, I had written a letter to my supervisors to request for funds to attend this training. I did this quickly because I knew the conference was approaching fast. Amazingly, my bosses agreed to pay for the full conference, including money for travel, meals, lodging, and the cost of the conference. It was remarkable. I got to meet many recreational therapists and to learn from the best.

I'm not going to go into the details of what I learned at this conference here. That would be information for another book. I do highly recommend that you get a copy of Canfield's *The Success Principles* book and read it twice so you can learn all the principals.

Read the book: *Do You!*

A Review of Russell Simmons with Chris Morrow's (2008) *Do You!: 12 Laws to Access the Power in You to Achieve Happiness and Success.* Published by Gotham.

Russell Simmons was dealing drugs as a teenager in Queens, New York during the 1970s, but he turned all that around by following his true passion for promoting hip-hop culture. Today, Simmons is often referred to as the "CEO of Hip-Hop." *USA Today* (2007, Sept. 9) acknowledged Simmons as being one of the 25 most influential people over the past 20 years. Russell was a creator of *Def Jam* record label and the fashion line, *Phat Farm.*

     Do You, is another one of my favorite all-time books. It had been on my "must-read book list" for a long time. It was recommended to me during Mark Victor Hansen's (2007) *Mega-Book Marketing University* seminar by Simmon's literary agent, Jillian Manus. I do caution that anytime someone has an invested interest in something to be careful about their recommendation. If a person who owned the shop was saying you need the item, it would be harder to trust because they have an interest in making a sell. But I listened to Jillian and I liked what she had to say about the book and decided I wanted to read it for myself. I like several hip-hop songs that play on the radio. I must admit, that I didn't really know much about Russell Simmons. Hip hop isn't my style of music. But the laws of success in his book can apply for anyone, anywhere. Simmons has become successful in music and writing and I recommend that people should read his book.

     Hidden and secret wisdom on becoming great is buried in *Do You!: 12 Laws to Access the Power in You to Achieve Happiness and Success* by Simmons. You'll never know what secrets it contains unless you read it. I'll share a few of the lessons that I learned from the book here. *Do You* is about being authentic and real. It is about being who you are and not trying to be a copy-cat or be a fake. Other people can see right through a person who is not real. Simmons catch phrase "*Do You*" is telling people to be themselves.

I am a healer, a therapist, and a writer. I enjoy hip-hop from time to time, but it is not what I'm all about. You may be all about hip-hop and that is okay. You've got to be yourself.

Simmons book, *Do You!: 12 Laws to Access the Power in You to Achieve Happiness and Success* is on the spiritual side, which I particularly enjoy as a healer. He argues that happiness comes first before success and money. He claims that there are no failures in life, but only quitters. The only time a person is really going to be a loser is if that person quits. You can be great as long as you persist and keep trying. It reminds me of one of my favorite movies, *Rocky*. People are inspired by *Rocky* because he always gets back up. He doesn't quit.

Giving is one of the main lessons in *Do You.* Simmons talks about giving it your best and being generous and giving more than is expected.

Simmons also argues that a person should surround herself (or himself) with the right people. This is where you go and seek out people who are great at what you want to be great at and learn from them. Surround yourself with a positive network.

You'll learn more on how to develop a positive social network of friends in an upcoming chapter.

"I've been blessed to find people who are smarter than I am, and they help me to execute my vision."

- Russell Simmons

Listen to Earl Nightingale

A review of Earl Nightingale's (1956) recording of
The Strangest Secret.
Published by: Nightingale-Conant

Earl Nightingale shares *The Strangest Secret* in the world, in his (1956) audio recording with the same title that sold over one-million copies. It is the only audio recording of a person simply talking to go platinum. Nightingale is considered one of the fathers of the self-improvement industry. His *Strangest Secret* is absolutely incredible. I recommend that you listen to it. Nightingale discusses three things: what is success, the power of thinking, and the power of giving.

"Success is the school teacher who is teaching because that's what he or she wants to do. A success is the entrepreneur who starts his own company because that was his dream."

- Earl Nightingale

Based on Nightingale's definition, I consider myself a success because I am a recreational therapist helping children and that was my predetermined goal. I also write self-improvement books as a healer because that is also my goal.

Thinking is the second main concept presented by Nightingale. He argues that a person becomes what she (or he) thinks about the most. A person moves in the direction of what she (or he) thinks about. William James, one of the founding fathers of psychology, said that humans only use 10% of their brain. Dr. Albert Schweitzer said that humans simply don't think.

A person can become great if they increase their self-awareness, positive thinking and use of their brain. How can they do that? They could use what scientists have learned about the brain. There are plenty of recent books on using more of the human mind. Here are four books that I suggest:

- *Out of our Minds: Learning to be More Creative* by Ken Robinson (2001)

- *A Whole New Mind, Why Right-Brainers Will Rule the Future* by Daniel Pink (2006)

- *Creative Visualization: Use the Power of Your Imagination to Create What You Want in Your Life* by Shakti Gawain (2002)

- *The Einstein Factor: A Proven New Method for Increasing Your Intelligence* by Win Wenger and Richard Poe (2002)

Reading is the key to discover hidden secret wisdom on becoming successful. You may want to read the books listed above.

What should you do now?

Focus on what you want to be great at. This is very important. Know what you want and keep your eye on the final goal. You could want anything. You might want a brand-new car. You might want to find a special significant other. You might want to be the world's best skier. You might want to climb Mt. Everest. You might want to own a resort at the beach. You might want to do many things. Only you know what you want to be great at doing.

Study those who are great. Learn all that you can from them. Especially, study those people who have gone before you and became great in the area that you want to be great. Build upon their successes. I've heard someone say that they stand on the shoulders of giants. Basically, what they're saying is that their accomplishments were possible because of the many great people who had gone before them. Why waste time trying to learn and discover things by trial and experience. That could take you many, many years to do. Why do that when you could learn faster and quicker from people who've already achieved success. Read about people who you find inspiring.

You may want to read the books by the four people discussed above:

- Sean Covey
- Jack Canfield
- Russell Simmons
- Earl Nightingale

You may also want to create a list of people who have inspired you. Seek out their books and read them.

The Hidden Secret Revealed in Chapter 4:

Learn wisdom by studying great people. Read everything you can about people who've inspired you.

*** Upcoming Attraction ***

Action is necessary. Knowing all the wisdom in the world alone won't make you great. You've got to take action. Getting a coach or mentor can help you take action. Continue reading the next chapter to learn how a coach or mentor can help you to become great.

Chapter 4 References

Canfield, J., & Switzer, J. (2007). *The Success
        Principles: How to Get from Where You Are to
        Where You Want to Be*. New York:
        HarperCollins.

Covey, S. (1998). *The 7 Habits Of Highly Effective
        Teens*. New York: Fireside.

Elliott, A. C. (1998). *A Daily Dose of the American
        Dream: Stories of Success, Triumph, and
        Inspiration*. Waco, TX: Thomas Nelson.

JackCanfield.Com (n.d.) *Meet Jack Canfield*. Retrieved
        April 2, 2009, from Web site:
        http://www.jackcanfield.com/page/?PageID=2

Morrow, C., & Simmons, R. (2008). *Do You!: 12 Laws
        to Access the Power in You to Achieve
        Happiness and Success*. New York: Gotham.

Nightingale, E. (1956). *The strangest secret*. [audio
        recording]. Nightingale-Conant.

USA Today. (2007, Sept. 3). *Most influential people*.
        Retrieved January 2009, from Web site:
        http://www.usatoday.com/news/top25-
        influential.htm

Chapter 5

The Truth About Teachers And Why You Need One to Become Great

"If you could find out what the most successful people did in any area and then you did the same thing over and over, you'd eventually get the same results they do."

- Brian Tracy

You need a mentor, coach, or teacher

Modeling is a type of social learning. Psychologists define it as learning through imitation of others. You could use modeling to become great. There is a greater guarantee of success when a person follows the path of someone who has already done it. You may find it useful to have a coach, mentor, or teacher who'll show you the way.

Who is my personal mentor?

I have many personal mentors. My father, Danny Pettry (senior) is one of them. He is a good man. He's taught me honesty, integrity, good work ethics and more because this is the type of person he is. I'm very fortunate to have had a father with good values, morals, and ethics. He's taught me a lot throughout my life. Many other family members have also helped me to get to where I am today, including my mother, grandparents, and teachers who have taught me over the years.

You could find a mentor in your profession. I discovered Dr. David Austin when I was an undergraduate student in Therapeutic Recreation at Marshall University (Huntington, West Virginia). Dr. Austin was the author of a book used for my first course titled: an introduction to therapeutic recreation. Dr. Austin had also created educational videos that were used for this class. He featured himself to help explain the introduction to therapeutic recreation.

Dr. Austin is an expert on recreational therapy practice (a.k.a. therapeutic recreation). He is a founding member of the American Therapeutic Recreation Association (ATRA) and has severed as a past-president. Dr. Austin developed the *Health Protection/ Health Promotion* model for recreational therapy practice. He is the author of several professional journal articles and many books, including my favorite in the profession: *Therapeutic Recreation: Processes and Techniques* (6th edition).

I consider Dr. Austin to be one of the several founders of modern recreational therapy practice. I am fortunate to say that he is one of my professional mentors. I seek his expert opinion and advice when needed.

Dr. Austin was a professor at Indiana University (Bloomington, Indiana), which is one of the leading schools for preparing recreational therapists. I had chosen to complete my master's degree at Indiana University because Dr. Austin was a professor there.

The "social psychology of therapeutic recreation" was one of my favorite courses that I had taken in graduate school. Dr. Austin was the instructor for this course. I was very fortunate to have had him as a teacher. This was the last course that he had taught for students in therapeutic recreation before he retired.

Today he is a professor emeritus. Dr. Austin continues to keep active in our profession. He writes a blog for recreational therapists that I follow: http://rt-blog.blogspot.com. He posts updated announcements regularly. I am an avid reader of his blog and I keep in contact with Dr. Austin through email.

Spend time with experts

My favorite motivational speaker, Jim Rohn, said: "You're the average of the five people you spend the most time with." I try my best to spend time with expert recreational therapists like Dr. Austin and other members of our professional organization: The American Therapeutic Recreation Association (ATRA).

Who do you spend the most time with? If they're all nurses then you're probably a nurse or another health practitioner. If they are all doing drugs then you're probably doing drugs. If their grades are all failing then yours are probably poor. If they are all gossip queens then as you can guess -- you're probably one, too.

How can you escape the mundane and become better? Surround yourself with people who are better than you. This is one reason why a coach or teacher can help. Find people who are great leaders in your area of interest or professional field.

My experience with social learning

Skateboarding was my passion during my teenager years. I loved it and I wanted to be the best skater ever. I skated every single day with my brother, Jimmy, and one of our neighbors, Chad. It was practically all we did. We got pretty good at skating. I tried to master the kickflip for my first year of skating, but couldn't land the trick. I didn't know how skaters did it. I watched the professional skaters in videos but just couldn't do it myself.

Adventurous skaters at our school invited Jimmy, Chad, and me to join them for skating. These skaters were amazing. I had seen new tricks that I hadn't seen before except in videos. Many of these skaters could land a kickflip easily. I learned from watching them do it and by imitating them. I started to land kickflips within days of watching and skating with them. It would have taken me a lot longer to master this trick had I continued to learn it on my own.

There is no doubt that I could have continued to become a great skater had I kept skating with people who were better than me.

I quit skating during my undergraduate college years. I wasn't willing to sacrifice my body to continue skating aggressively. I had dislocated my left shoulder, broken a wrist, sprained an ankle, and had numerous scrapes during my teenage years. Tony Hawk is one of the world's best-known skaters. Hawk has gone through many injuries to get to where he is today. Hawk has had two concussions, lost his front teeth, and broken an elbow as a result of skateboarding according to (AskMen.Com, no date). He's a great skater because he is passionate and dedicated.

Learning from people who are better than you is a great technique for becoming great. Your coach, mentor, or teacher does not have to have the title of "coach" or "teacher." They could simply be a person who is skilled at doing something. You could learn from this person by watching, imitating, and asking questions.

Take a class

Ice-skating, painting, singing, and many other things can be learned from taking a class. There are instructors who teach everything and anything. You could benefit from hiring a teacher to teach you the skill. If you truly want to become great at doing something, it may be beneficial to find a teacher who is successful at what you want to do.

An example is: If you want to become a nurse then take nursing education courses. Classes for nurses are offered at your local college or university. College can be a big expense. There are ways to help find money for college, such as loans, work study, paying for one class at a time. The benefits of education far outweigh the cost of an education.

Some classes (like mechanics) may not be offered at your local college or university. These skills could be taught at a technical or vocational school. You could also hire a person to teach you. Ask someone if you can shadow and observe them for a while.

Hire a fitness trainer if you want to be a body builder or if you want to get in shape. Hire a piano teacher if you want to learn to play the piano. Take acting lessons or a drama course if you want to be an actress (or actor). If you don't want to be anything then don't do anything. Don't read this book unless you want to achieve greatness. This book is written exclusively for people who want to become great. It isn't for the quitters.

Attend a live training or seminar

Wisdom can be revealed from attending seminars. You may learn something important from attending them. Don't put if off any longer. You know that you want to be great. Go and attend a live training. It could be a little costly, but it is well worth the investment. You won't regret it.

Healing people is my passion. I want to be the greatest recreational therapist that I can be. I've had the opportunity to attend several seminars for recreational therapists in Kansas City, Missouri, Greenville, South Carolina and Washington D.C. These were awesome opportunities. I got to meet recreational therapists from nearly every state. I keep in touch with many of them today by email. Training sessions at these seminars taught the most updated techniques for effective recreational therapy practice.

You probably don't want to become a recreational therapist, so I won't go into the details about these conferences here. You know what you want to do with your life. Attend a seminar in that field.

Consider e-learning and online classes

Online learning is exploding in interest because people can do it easily from the comfort of home. Classes are being offered online for many things. These include success workshops, foreign languages, business classes, and many more.

You could do a quick online search in the area of your interest to see what is offered online. Online learning is the way of the future. You'll also increase your skills with computers and technology, too. Some courses can be completed online. Unfortunately, you don't get the live face-to-face contact with people when you take an online class.

All subjects can't be learned online. Many subjects require an extensive course study and may take several years of classroom study. Some courses also require an internship. Online courses could offer you a gateway into the learning experience. Online classes could be a first step to discovering more.

Notice: Recreational therapists and allied professionals can earn continuing education units (CEUs) by taking classes through my online self-study program. Go to this link for more information:

www.DannyPettry.com

Use audio to become great

Repetition, repetition, and repetition are the real three "Rs" in education. People learn best when they repeat things. Listening to courses on audio is effective because you can re-play it. Many of the self-improvement gurus have their own programs on C.D. that you could use. You can even download these audio courses to your iPod. My personal iPod includes trainings from success gurus including, Jim Rohn, Earl Nightingale, Jack Canfield, Mark Victor Hansen, and Anthony Robbins.

A C.D. is a great way to learn when you can't attend a live training or seminar. Professionals often record their live seminars on C.D. If you can't attend the live trainings then you could buy an audio recording at more affordable price. This is my little secret to getting wisdom presented at live seminars that cost thousands of dollars to attend.

The Hidden Secret Revealed in Chapter 5:

Get a personal teacher, coach, or mentor as soon as possible.

*** Upcoming Attraction ***

Do you want to discover how movies can help you to become great? If so, then continue reading the next chapter.

Chapter 5 References

AskMen.Com. (no date.) *Interview: Tony Hawk.* Retrieved April 1, 2009, from: http://www.askmen.com/celebs/interview/28b_t ony_hawk_interview.html

"Do teachers still get paid if I don't learn anything?"

© 2009 by Jonny Hawkins. Reprinted with permission. All rights reserved.

Chapter 6

These Movies Inspire Greatness in About 90-Minutes-A-Day

"You are your own scriptwriter and the play is never finished, no matter what your age or position in life."

- Denis Waitley

Cinema therapy

Healing and self-improvement can be achieved through the use of watching movies. Cinema therapy is a technique in which a person is prescribed to watch certain movies in order to have personal growth. Some recreational therapists use cinema therapy as a technique to help people to become better.

Several cinema therapy books have been published. Three popular ones that I use as a recreational therapist to help children, teens, and adults include:

- *The Motion Picture Prescription: Watch This Movie and Call Me in the Morning: 200 Movies to Help You Heal Life's Problems* by Gary Solomon (1995).

- *Talking Pictures: A Parent's Guide to Using Movies to Discuss Ethics, Values, and Everyday Problems with Children* by Ronald Madison and Corey Schmidt. (2001).

- *E-Motion Picture Magic: A Movie Lover's Guide to Healing and Transformation* by Brigit Wolz. (2004).

You may want to consider reading some of these books to determine what movies would be best for you.

The idea of using movies as a tool for healing, personal growth, and self-development is excellent. A movie doesn't take long to watch. There are hidden themes and meanings in most movies that could help a person to grow. The use of movies is a lot like the use of books for healing (bibliotherapy). There are so many movies out there that you're bound to find one that could help you to achieve personal growth. A quick review of the three books I listed above could easily help you find the movie that is right for you.

Why do people watch movies?

Enjoyment is the primary reason that people watch movies. During the great depression, people in U.S. had to give up a lot of things because of lack of money. Movies were one thing that people did not give up. People continued to go to the cinemas to watch movies during the depression because it was a healthy escape from reality. It allowed people to experience happiness when times were rough, tough, and gloomy. People watched movies for entertainment back then, too.

Why should a person watch movies?

Emotions cause people to change. People do not change because of rational thinking alone. People change when they feel strong compelling emotions. This is one reason commercials are like mini-movies. They're attempting to get people to buy through the use of emotions.

Movies can cause a person to experience a wide-range of emotions. People laugh, smile, cry, and even become angry during movies. Movies are realistic and lifelike. They can cause emotions in people.

Movies can teach many valuable lessons on friendship, aging, values, morals, ethics, drugs and alcohol, sickness, death and dying, and so much more.

Movies can do more than just provide a person with entertainment. They can help a person to have life-changing experiences. They can inspire and encourage people to change their life. Watching the right movie at the right time could do wonders for a person. People identify with the characters in movies. Naturally, I want you to be inspired towards greatness. I'll suggest four movies that could inspire you here:

Movie # 1: Watch *It's a Wonderful Life*

A Review of Frank Capra's [director and producer] (1946) motion picture, *It's a Wonderful Life.*

Purpose of life is a very important thing to understand. All people have a purpose. Even if you don't know what your purpose is yet, know this: you have one. You've got some mission or goal to accomplish before you die. You may already know what it is. You may not know what you need to do yet. Regardless, you've got a reason to be here.

George Bailey is a fictional character who I admire. He is the star character in the (1946) black and white movie, *It's a Wonderful Life.* George has dreams to become an explorer from an early age. He wanted to see the world and do many things.

George was a good guy who did the right thing. His father owned a small loan company in the fictional town of Bedford Falls. George felt like he had to take the responsibility of the loan company after the death of his father. He gave up his dream of becoming a world explorer.

The richest man in town, Mr. Potter was selfish. He wanted to buy out the small loan company after George's father passed away so that he could prevent good people from getting loans. Good ol' George Bailey steps up and takes over the company after his father's death and helps many people in Bedford Falls.

Bad things happen in life from time to time. George's uncle loses money that belongs to the loan company. Mr. Potter, the richest man in town finds the money at the bank. Mr. Potter knows who the money belongs to, but he does not return it to George Bailey or his uncle. Mr. Potter decides to keep the money and call the police accusing George of using the money for gambling or some other self-interest.

It is a tough time for George. He realizes that his life insurance would be worth more for him dead then alive. He thinks about committing suicide and ending it all. But, George has a guardian angel. The angle shows him just how important his life really is. The angel takes George and shows him what the world would be like had he never been born at all. It is hard to imagine how one life could touch so many people. The movie showed how important good ol' George Baily was to his family, friends, and community. Realize this: you're just as

important as George. You have a purpose, too.
Deepak Chopra, a spiritual writer says it this way:

> "Everyone is here because he or she has a place to
> fill, and every piece must fit itself into the big
> jigsaw puzzle."

Watching a movie like this could help you to
see that you have a purpose just like George Bailey.
You are meant to do something in this life. Do
whatever it is to the best of your ability and strive to
be great at doing it.

- **Movie # 2: Watch *Good Will Hunting***

A Review of Gus Van Sant [director] and Matt
Damon and Ben Affleck's [writers] (1997) motion
picture, *Good Will Hunting*

Free will to do what you want to do in life is
wonderful. You can have, be, or do anything you
want. Ken Robinson in his (2001) book*, Out of Our
Minds: Learning to be Creative,* discussed a girl
who was good at playing piano, but didn't enjoy it.
Robinson says: "being good at something isn't a
good enough reason to spend you life doing it."
Dale Carnegie, author of *How to Win Friends and
Influence People* had once said: "You never achieve
success unless you like what you are doing."

In the (1997) fictional movie, *Good Will
Hunting*, a young boy, Will, mops floors at MIT. He
could have chosen any job in the world, but he
decides to clean the floors at this major institute of

higher learning. Why? Will is a natural-born math prodigy. He solves a math problem on the chalk board one night while cleaning. College students couldn't solve this equation. Will did in one night what most students would require a full year to do. The math professor tracks Will down and discovers he is in trouble with the law. Will had had a bad life. He suffered abuse as a child and grew up in an orphanage with several other boys. He has a fear of going for what he really wants.

The math professor agrees to watch Will and pay for therapy services in order to keep Will out of jail. The math professor has a desire to control Will and force him into a mathematician career.

Will goes through several therapists until he finds the right one. Sean, a therapist played by Robin Williams shows Will that Will, himself, is in charge of his own life. He shows Will that he can choose what he wants to do with his life. Will decides to go for what he wants. Will, although a math prodigy, decides that he doesn't want to be a mathematician. He decides to go to California to be with a girl who he loves.

You can live your life the way you want to live it. You decide what is right for you. Someone may attempt to force you into doing a certain type of career or job, but you don't have to do it. Follow your dreams.

You've got free will to decide what kind of job you want to do. You'll be greater at doing something you love compared to doing something you do not love.

- **Movie # 3: Watch *"The Pistol - Birth of a Legend"***

A Review of Frank C. Schroder [director] and
Darrell Campbell and Peter Maravich's [writers]
(1991) motion-picture,
Pistol – The Birth of a Legend

Dedication to dreams can make a person become great. The movie, *The Pistol* is the true story of Pete Maravich, a National Basketball Association (NBA) Great. This is a must see movie even if you're not into sports or basketball. The lessons in this movie can inspire you to become great in whatever it is that you want to become great.

"Pistol" got his nickname because he could shoot a basketball from the hip like a gun-shooter. Pete knew he wanted to be a professional basketball player at an early age. He spent hours practicing. He played basketball anytime he had a chance. He lived, breathed, and slept basketball. He was fortunate because he had a great coach, too. His father was a basketball coach who was teaching him how to become a great player. As discussed in the previous chapter: a coach could help you to become great.

Pete lived for basketball. Pete told people that he had his heart set on playing basketball for the West Virginia University (WVU) Mountaineers (one of my favorite teams). However, Pete went to Louisiana State University (LSU) to play, partly because his father was the varsity coach there at the time and he was offered a position. Knowing people in key places can help you to get a position, but keeping these positions requires talent and dedication, which Pete had. Pistol Pete went on to become one of the greatest basketball players ever after graduating from LSU.

In the movie, Pete likes a girl in school. She says she wants to be an actress. Pete asked, if she was going to be a great actress. She said, "No." Pete asked: "why would you do something unless you're going to be great at it?" He makes a good point. Why do anything unless you're going to be the best that you can be at it?

Watch movies based on true stories like Pistol Pete because they are inspirational.

- **Movie # 4: Watch *October Sky***

A Review of Joe Johnston [director] and Homer Hickan [author] and Lewis Colick [screenplay writer] (1999) motion-picture, *October Sky*.

Desire to do great things is buried in all of us. All people have a want to live the life of her (or his) own dreams. The movie, *October Sky* is based on the true story of Homer Hickam. In the 1950s, a boy like Homer who lived in Coalwood, West Virginia was destined for one thing. He would live his full life in a little town working as a coal miner. Homer didn't want to live this life. His father was a dedicated coal miner who loved working in the mines. Homer's father wanted him to follow his footsteps and become a miner, too. Homer had his own hopes and dreams. He desired to be something different.

Sputnick was the first satellite launched into space by America's arch-enemy. At the time it was the Russians. Young, Homer watched the satellite as it flew over the West Virginia sky. Homer knew then that he wanted to learn about space. He studied rockets and learned everything he could. He got a science scholarship that helped him to get out of Coalwood at a time when the only kids to get scholarships were football players. Homer went on to become employed for NASA. It is a true story of following ones own hopes and dreams. Had he not followed his dreams he wouldn't be where he is today. Had he did what his father said; he would be working in a coal mine today. His life would be average, but instead Homer decided to live a great life and to do what he desired. He had written his life story in a book called, *Rocket Boys*, which is the basis for the movie *October Sky*. Homer said his dad was his hero. I imagine he said this because he saw that his dad was a person who lived his dreams. Homer realized that his dad loved his job as a coal miner. His dad had passion and loved being in the mines. Homer lived his life the same way as his father. He followed his passion for science and rockets and went on to work for NASA.

Movies that motivate

So far, I've discussed two fictional movies that could inspire you to become great. These include: *It's a Wonderful Life* and *Good Will Hunting*. I've also discussed two movies based on true stories that could inspire you to become great. These include: *The Pistol: Birth of a Legend* and *October Sky*. These are just a few movies that you should consider watching. You should seek out inspiring movies, especially ones based on true-stories. Write the names of these movies down on your list of must-watch movies, if you've not viewed them already. Two of my personal favorite movies on greatness include the (1995) HBO movie, *Truman*, based on the life of my favorite U.S. President, Harry S. Truman and the (2005) movie, *Warm Springs*, based on the life of President Franklin D. Roosevelt. You could also watch documentaries on famous people who have became great. Interesting information can be found hidden in documentaries. They can present you with many ideas that you've never even thought about before.

Caution

Be careful about what you view on television. I am picky about what I watch on television. I enjoy good movies, but I am careful not to just waste time watching endless television shows that are useless. I find myself falling into this habit from time to time. I doubt that anyone ever became great by just sitting home and watching television. A single man never met a perfect person to ask out on a date while staying home and watching re-runs. An exciting life does not happen by watching other people on television having their moments.

Television can be used for good purposes. I do warn you to watch how you spend your time. You may have completed the exercise in your complimentary journal regarding how you spend your time. This was also covered in chapter 1 (on self-discovery). If you've not done so already, download and print your complimentary journal at this link:

www.hiddensecretwisdom.com/bonus

You may realize that you spend 40 hours or more watching television a week. Think about what you could do with your life if you dedicated at least half of that (20 hours) a week to a new skill or activity. You could get in shape and lose weight if you exercised that much. You could write several novels if you used that time to write. You could learn to speak Spanish if you dedicated yourself. In fact, you could become great at many things if you use your time wisely.

One of my favorite authors, Denis Waitly, author of the *Psychology of Winning*, said during Mark Victor Hansen's (2007) *Mega Book Marketing University Training* that he had written his book during "Prime Time." This was his evenings and weekends. He used this time to be productive to write his bestselling book opposed to watching others on television. I've imitated Denis Waitly's process by writing this book during my own evenings and weekends opposed to wasting time watching television.

The Hidden Secret Revealed in Chapter 6:

Learn secrets to become great by watching inspirational, life-changing, movies.

*** Upcoming Attraction ***

What good would it do if you're the most successful person in the world, but you're not happy? Would it be worth being great if you were depressed or upset? Happiness is needed in order to truly feel great. Continue reading the next chapter if you're interested in discovering secret wisdom on how to become happy, great, and successful.

Chapter 6 References

Capra, F. (director & producer). (1946). *It's a wonderful life* [Motion picture]. United States: Liberty Films.

Johnston, J. (director), Hickam, H. (author), & Colick, L. (screenplay writer). (1999). *October sky* [Motion picture]. United States: Universal Pictures

Robinson, K. (2001). *Out of our minds: learning to be more creative.* Capstone.

Sant, G. (director), Damon, M. (writer), & Affleck, B. (writer). (1998*). Good will hunting* [Motion picture]. United States: Miramax Films.

Schroder, F. (director), Campbell, D. (writer), & Mavarich, P. (writer). (1991). *Pistol – the birth of a legend* [Motion picture]. United States: L.A. Film Partners.

Waitley, D. (speaker). (2007). *Mark victor hansen's mega book marketing university* [C.D.]. M. V. Hansen & Associates.

"It doesn't work on *that*, son."

© 2009 by Jonny Hawkins. Reprinted with permission.
All rights reserved.

Chapter 7

New Discovery Reveals How Being Happy Will Help You to Become Great!

"Success is not the key to happiness. Happiness is the key to success. If you love what you are doing, you will be successful."

- Albert Schweitzer

Feel happy

Greatness depends on happiness.
Many people believe that they'll feel great and
happy once they've achieved something. They have
the idea that getting a lot of money, a nice car, new
toys, the richest boyfriend, or most attractive
girlfriend will make them happy. This isn't the way
to happiness. It is the other way around.

Happiness comes first. It is a prerequisite to
becoming great. If you're not happy then you're not
going to become great and successful. You're not
going to achieve your goals with a negative mental
attitude. It isn't going to work that way. A person
must be happy in order to become successful.
Happiness leads to greatness.

Warning: A person who is waiting to
accomplish something before they can feel happy
and great will always be empty inside. They'll
constantly want to get something else in order to be
happy. Nothing they achieve will be good enough.
Happiness must be present first.

Good news: Research studies show how a
person can become happier. Scientists have been
studying depression and ways to help people feel
happy. You can apply this information to your own
life in order to feel happier.

Read *Happy for No Reason*

A Review of
Happy for No Reason: 7 Steps to Being Happy From the Inside Out by Marci Shimoff with Carol Kline (2009). Published by: TS Production LLC.

Marci Shimoff is one of the leading experts on happiness. She is featured in the documentary, *The Secret* and she is a co-author of *Chicken Soup for the Woman's Soul*. She knows what it takes to be happy and shares how to be happy with others.

Marci Shimoff covers seven basic principles on how a person can become happy in her (2009) book. These concepts and ideas are grounded in research. I highly recommend you to read her full book to get all the gems of information that you can. Here is a brief overview of the seven principles Shimoff presents in her book:

- Be responsible for your own happiness. You're the only person who can do this for you. It is simply your job to be happy.

- Change your thoughts if you need to. Based on my personal experiences as a recreational therapist, I've worked with many children at the hospital who have poor thinking patterns. We call this "stinky thinking." We teach these children how to have "oscar thinking." Some of the negative thinking patterns include: "blaming" others for things that are really their own responsibility and "poor-me" where they see everything as bad.

- Uncover your spiritual side. Find meaning in the world and for your life. Learn to listen to your inner voice.

- Live a life full of love. Focus on love. Practice doing good, loving deeds.

- Take care of your body. Physical health can lead to happiness. Plus, it is the only body you get.

- Do things which you are passionate about in your life. As a recreational therapist, I highly recommend that you participate in meaningful activities.

- Build a strong social support network. Make many friends so you'll have people who you could call upon in times of need.

I highly recommend that you read Shimoff's (2009) book *Happy for No Reason*.

Just forgive

Release negative feelings in order to be happy. Holding onto anger will only hurt you. A person who forgives quite simply lets things go.

Hale Dwoskin is the author of the (2003) book called, *The Sedona Method*. It is the process of letting go. Dwoskin says to hold a pencil or an ink pen very tightly. Imagine that you're holding onto all of those negative feelings. Continue holding the ink pen. After a while, holding the pencil or ink pen begins to feel normal. It doesn't feel like you're holding it. It is just there. Let things go. Practice it. Just drop the pencil or ink pen. It is that simple. Dropping unwanted negative feelings can be just as simple, too, according to Dwoskin.

"I will never forgive her, I won't," said a little girl at the hospital, where I work. As always, I ask, what seems to be the problem? She replied that one of her female peers had given her a "dirty face." This may be true. I didn't see her peer give her a negative facial expression. Her strong reactions led me to believe it was true. Both girls are depressed. They had both came from dysfunctional homes where they had been physically abused. Deep down, they are both children who are hurt. Letting go of things they can't change in the past helps them move forward. I told her to "just let it go." Don't let someone else have power over your feelings.

Hurt and anger are tough emotions. Having hard feelings like this over a long period of time is hard on a person's physical and mental well-being. The only way to feel better is to forgive and let go. I understand that it is easier said than done.

I apply "letting go" to simple things in my life. An example is if a co-worker is in a bad mood and they took it out on me. Rather than to get angry, I just let it go. I know my co-worker didn't have anything against me. She was just having a bad moment. Later, things were fine because I let it go. Our work relationship is still friendly. Many of the children who I provide therapy for say hurtful things. I don't take it personally either. I just let it go.

Use Positive Words

Hal Urban is the author of the (2004) book, *Positive Words, Powerful Results: Simple Ways to Honor, Affirm, and Celebrate Life*. Urban discusses an elderly group who willingly participated in a scientific study. They were randomly selected to enter into one of two rooms to receive instructions on how to perform an activity. They were to complete the activity in a different room that was at the end of a long hall. In room "A" the instructor used words in his talk that included: weak, fragile, old, forgetful, and other words that are associated with aging. In room "B" the instructor used different words that were associated with aging. These words included: wise, experienced, strong-willed, and many other positive words. After the training, seniors in both rooms were allowed to walk down the long hallway to the other room to perform the activity. The activity at the end of the hall wasn't what the researchers were studying. They studied how long it would take for each individual to walk down the hallway. As you guessed, the people who received instructions from room "B," walked faster to the activity room at the end of the hallway compared to seniors who attended the training in room "A." The power of language and words is astonishing.

I try my best to use positive words and language while working with children at the hospital. I understand that what I say has a strong impact on them. I refrain from using words like "bad." Instead of saying "bad," I would say, "not-so-good." This is called the "Pink Elephant" concept. If I told you to NOT think about a pink elephant wearing a purple dress while walking across a high wire with a little yellow umbrella, the funny image would still cross your mind. If I told a child to "stop being bad," the child would hear the words "being bad" and think of herself (or himself) as "bad." Instead, I'd try to say, "Maybe that wasn't the best thing you've done or maybe that wasn't the nicest thing to do. What could you do that would be better, nicer, or kinder next time? The child hears positive words like *nice, best, better and kinder* when this approach is used.

Death, terror, hate, mad, ugly, and similar negative words are listed on one sheet of page in Urban's (2004) book. At the bottom of the page is a question: "how do you feel after reading these words?" Naturally, you'd feel "not-so-good." I don't even show this list anymore after a child began to cry once. These words were "triggers" for him. They reminded him of his abuse and it triggered strong emotions.

Smile, happy, puppy, sunshine, rainbows, stars, and other positive words are listed on a different page in Urban's (2004) book. These words are associated with feelings of happiness and good-times. This list of words is like an antidote for the first set of words. As you guessed, a person feels a lot more positive after reading the second list. The same question is featured at the bottom: "how do you feel after reading these words?" Hal Urban's (2004) book is filled with evidenced on the power of positive words. If you want to be great then start using powerful and positive words in your thinking and every day language.

Water and words

Positive words can influence water. A breakthrough study by Japanese scientist Masaru Emoto has shown what words can do to water in his (2007) book, *The Miracle of Water.*

Dr. Emoto (2007) wanted to determine what happens when water crystallizes with the use words. Emoto would have words written on bottles of water. He spoke the same words to the bottle of water, too. Emoto would freeze the water and then watch how it crystallizes. Water turned into beautiful crystals when music with positive words was played. Positive words such as "I love you" and "gratitude" written on the bottle and spoken to created beautiful crystals despite the language spoken, too. Negative words, such as, "I hate you" formed incomplete/ unattractive crystals compared to the ones with positive words. Google search "Emoto Crystals" to see up-close microscope pictures of the crystallized water.

Reality is created by thoughts. This is the hypothesis of Dr. Masaru Emoto. Our complete reality is determined by the way we think.

Water is a major part of human life. It makes up about 70% of the human body. I question Emoto's study and would like to see more research for consistency. I believe this study has some truth to it. Imagine what your thoughts are doing to you. If you're thinking positive thoughts then you are creating health and a better physical body. If you're thinking negative thoughts then your mental and physical health will be poor.

Humor

Laughter is the best medicine according to the old motto. There is plenty of evidence that shows laughter can result in a more happier and positive mood. One cancer survivor featured in Rhonda Byrne's (2006) documentary, *The Secret* claims that she healed her cancer through the use of watching funny movies and having laughter in her life.

A Joke a Day Keeps the Doctor Away is an amazing book with jokes by Bob Phillips (2008). It is illustrated by one of my favorite cartoonist, Jonny Hawkins. I share the appropriate jokes at work with the children. Bob Phillips has several joke books for children that are appropriate as well.

Humor therapy

Patch Adams is a real doctor. You may have heard of the (1998) movie with the same title. Patch Adams was played by the actor, Robin Williams in this movie.

Dr. Patch Adams had opened Gesundheit Institute in West Virginia. The word "gesundheit" is German. It means to wish a person good health. Some people say "gesundheit" opposed to "bless you" after a person sneezes. The Gesundheit Institute provides health services for people who can't afford it.

Patch Adams is known for dressing as a clown to cheer people up at hospitals. He treats people as real people. A newer Gesundheit Institute is being planned for West Virginia. It will include: arts, crafts, recreation, and other forms of alternative/ holistic therapies for healing according to (Wikipedia.com, 2009).

Research studies have demonstrated to us that humor and other recreational therapies have a strong, positive impact on health and wellness.

Spend time with positive people

Uplifting and happy people can help you to feel happy. If you're around upbeat people it will rub off on you. Happiness is contagious. Imagine a room where many people are laughing and having a good time. Even if you don't know what they are laughing at, you'll be inspired to smile. You might start giggling yourself even though you don't know why they're laughing and having a good time. Have you heard of the game "ha?" It is a group game that encourages laughter. The first person says "ha." The second person says it twice: "ha, ha." The third person says it three times, "ha, ha, ha." Eventually, the whole group breaks out in uncontrolled laughter - based on my experiences. Laughter and happiness can be contagious.

Spending time with inspirational people is much better than dwelling in misery, whining, complaining, and having a pity party. I believe all people know at least one person who has that negative attitude that brings everyone else down with them. Try to avoid them. If you can't avoid them, then try to be around this person when she (or he) is at her (or his) best. Maybe your happiness will make them feel more upbeat and happy.

I believe that all people in the world are good people at heart. My theory is that people only behave in not-so-good ways when they are experiencing strong uncomfortable emotions. These could be fear, anger, jealously, etc. A person who is feeling these strong emotions could be compelled to act in ways that are not-so-noble.

Gratitude journal

This is a journal where a person keeps a written record of things she (or he) is glad about. This journal can vary. It could be a book of blank pages where a person can draw or cut out magazines pictures and keep a collage of things to be happy about in life. It could be a scrapbook, where a person takes pictures and keeps mementos of things to be happy about like movie ticket-stub or other items.   It could be a journal with lined pages.

Focusing on the positive could be easier with a tool, like a gratitude journal. A person only has to re-read the journal or look through her (or his) scrapbook to be reminded of all the positive things to be glad about.

Children who are upset are often obvious. Their body language says "I'm angry." I can see it in their faces. They fold their arms. I ask them, what are you glad about today? They'll hardly reply back, or say, "nothing." I prompt them. Are you glad you have eyes so that you can see? Are you glad you've got fingers so that you can write, eat, and play video games? I know people who are blind and people who can't use their arms or legs. You could decide to be glad about what you do have.

Sometimes this does not work because the child will still say, "no, I'm not glad about that either." I don't get into power struggles. When I come across situations like this, I simply say, "Okay, you can at least be glad that you're aware that you're not glad about anything. Who's next?" Sometimes by the end of the session the child wants to share something after all.

I think about gratitude often. I feel very fortunate to have so many wonderful things in life. I have a loving family. I have a career that I love to do, helping children. I have food to eat, a warm bed for sleeping, friends whom I can call on, and so much more. I'm very fortunate. Why don't you make a list of things you are grateful for today. You may be surprised at the many wonderful things on your list.

Sometimes I think about gratitude when I eat. I had read *Anne Frank's Diary of a Young Girl*. Anne was a victim of the holocaust. She had kept a diary of her daily events while living/ hiding in an attic with her family so the Nazis wouldn't find them. Time there was unbearable at times. Her family was cramped in a small space with another family and a doctor who were all in hiding. Food was scarce. Sometimes when I'm eating I feel so fortunate to have food. I think about Anne and her diary. I wish I could somehow reach out to her and her family and give them food. I feel like I personally know Anne from reading her diary. She is one of my all-time favorite people. It deeply saddens me that she passed away in a concentration camp weeks before it was liberated. There is a chance she'd still be alive today. She'd be an elder woman who would have had many life experiences. Anne wanted to be a writer. She would have given this world many wonderful books, of this I am certain.

The major point that I'm getting to is to be grateful for what you have. Make use of your talents and abilities. Don't take them for granted. Be grateful that you have them and use them to make the world a better place. Write that book that Anne Frank wasn't able to write because she had passed away early. None of us know when our final day will be so make use of time now. Learn to play guitar if that is what you want to do. Learn to rock-climb or do whatever it is that you want to do in life. Do it now because you might not get the chance to do so tomorrow. Look for the good things in life and keep a happy, positive attitude.

You can download a free copy of the gratitude journal that I use for helping children and teens. It is good for adults to use as well. It is simple to use. Go here to download and print your copy today:

---

www.hiddensecretwisdom.com/bonus

Change your thinking

Feeling good is what happiness is all about. It may just require a slight shift in your thinking. Dr. David Burns presents techniques for happiness in his (1999) book, *Feeling Good: The New Mood Therapy.*

Cognitive-Behavioral Therapy (CBT) is the treatment that Dr. Burns presents. This is a type of treatment that is based on changing thought patterns. It consists of getting rid of negative thinking that a person has developed. It is a type of treatment that doesn't require medication. Right at the start of the book, Dr. Burns identifies a list of "faulty thinking patterns" that result in negative feelings. Changing these thought patterns could help a person to feel better. I recommend that you rent the book from your local library to get the full benefits on how to change negative thoughts into positive feelings. It includes a self-assessment checklist for you to determine if you're depressed.

Have some fun

Activities that you enjoy could cause you to feel happy. Participating in a variety of activities that you love to do could be an excellent way to feel pleasure and excitement in your life. These activities could include anything. You could start a garden, take karate, join a book club, start swimming, take a walk and enjoy nature, draw a picture, start playing a guitar, call a friend, or do anything fun.

Enjoy life to its fullest. Participate in a variety of activities that make you happy. Don't let time waste away while doing nothing. Activities are one of the greatest keys to greatness. If you continue participating in any activity you'll continue to get better and better at it. You'll become great at it if you do it for long enough. A person can't do one push-up in a year and say she (or he) has become fit. A person would have to do about 30 minutes of exercise a day. One day working the upper part of the body and the next day working the lower part of the body is recommended. There are 52 weeks in a year. If a person exercises for 30 minutes for 5 days of a week for 52 weeks, then she'll have exercised a total of 7,800 hours. A person who does that much exercise compared to a person who does one push-up will be in far greater shape. The same holds true for anything that you want to become great at. You must give it your best.

The Hidden Secret Revealed in Chapter 7:

You must feel happy most of the time before you can become great.

*** Upcoming Attraction ***

Do you want to discover how using your leisure time can make you great? Would you like to know how recreation can make your life better and greater? If so, continue reading the next chapter to learn more secret wisdom on becoming great.

Chapter 7 References

Burns, D. (1999). *Feeling Good: The New Mood Therapy Revised and Updated*. Boston: Avon.

Byrne, R. (Producer), & Heroit, D. (Director). (2006). *The Secret* [Motion Picture]. Australia: TS Production LLC.

Dwoskin, H. (2003). *The Sedona Method: Your Key to Lasting Happiness, Success, Peace and Emotional Well-Being*. Novato, CA: Sedona Press.

Emoto, M. (2007). *The Miracle of Water*. New York: Atria.

Frank, A. (1993). *Anne Frank: The Diary of a Young Girl (Mass Market Paperback)*. New York: Bantam.

Phillips, B. (2008). *A Joke a Day Keeps the Doctor Away*. Eugene: Harvest House Publishers.

Shimoff, M. & Kline, C. (2009). *Happy for No Reason: 7 Steps to Being Happy from the Inside Out*. New York City: Free Press.

Urban, H. (2004). *Positive Words, Powerful Results: Simple Ways to Honor, Affirm, and Celebrate Life*. New York: Fireside.

Wikipedia.com. (n.d.). *Patch Adams*. Retrieved April 23,2009, from: http://en.wikipedia.org/wiki/Patch_Adams

"Dad, can I borrow the keys to happiness?"

© 2007 Jonny Hawkins

Jonny Hawkins
P.O. Box 188
Sherwood, MI 49089
269-432-8071
Code# JH-21628

Notice that the father is holding a book in his hands. He has tons of books on the shelf. Maybe books are the key to happiness

© 2009 by Jonny Hawkins. Reprinted with permission. All rights reserved.

Danny Pettry Quotes

Read, read, read
if you want
to succeed.
- Danny Pettry

How to discover wisdom:
Read.

How to become great at anything:
Take action. Apply what you've learned.

Chapter 8

Here's How To Become Great In Your Spare Time - And Have Fun Doing It!

"Recreation's purpose is not to kill time, but to make life, not to keep a person occupied, but to keep them refreshed; not to offer an escape from life, but to provide a discovery of life."

- Author Unknown

Do something fun

Greatness can be achieved during your leisure through your recreational pursuits. You could become great at your passion and hobbies. This would give you a huge boost in self-confidence, too. This is a fun way to become great because you'll love being involved in the recreational activity.

Many people become great in leisure and recreation activities because they're dedicated and persistent. Here is a list of people who have become professionals in their recreational pursuits.

- John Comer is a professional skateboarder

- Bethany Hamilton is professional surfer

- Shea Cowart a professional track and field athlete

- Leanne Beetham is a professional painter

If they can do it, then so can you

Did you realize that all of the people listed above have a disability, but they are still achieving greatness? I'm very inspired by people who live great lives despite limitations. They are living miracles.

Here is some information about each of these amazing and inspiring individuals:

John Comer is in his 30s and he is a professional skateboarder. I first discovered him in a (1995) skateboarding video called, *The Best of 411 Video Magazine, Volume II.* He had a below the knee amputee since he was young. Comer has been skating since he was ten-years-old because it was something fun-to-do. Comer competes in vert, (the half-pipe shaped ramp) skateboarding contests and ranks high in all of them. He competes with skaters without disabilities. There is a (2004) documentary about his life, called, *Never Been Done* that you may be interested in watching. For more information on Comer go to this website: www.neverbeendone.com

Bethany Hamilton was surfing on Halloween morning in 2003. A great tiger shark had bit off her arm. It was a horrible tragedy. Bethany lost her arm altogether. Bethany shared her life story in her (2006) book, *Soul Surfer: A True Story of Faith, Family, and Fighting to Get Back on the Board.* This is an amazing story about determination and being great. Today, she is in her late teenage years and she continues to surf professionally. Bethany is winning many awards. She is featured in the DVD, *Heart of a Soul Surfer.* For information, go here: www.heartofasoulsurfer.com

Shea Cowart is a sprinter. I first saw a picture of her in a magazine in 2002 and noticed that she had prosthetic legs that were designed for running track. As a student in a recreational therapy degree program at the time, I was amazed at the picture of Shea. I thought it was awesome that she was doing something great with her life. According to (Wikipedia, 2009) Shea had meningococcemia at the age of six and lost both of her legs below the knee as a result. She won two gold medals and broke the world record in the 2000 Paralympics Games.

Leanne Beetham is an amazing painter. Her pictures are realistic and breathtaking. People pay hundreds of dollars for her paintings. You'd never know that Leanne is unable to use her arms or legs by looking at her paintings. Here is the fun part. She paints with her mouth. She was born with arthrogryposis syndrome. I'd love to post her artwork here, but I've not obtained the copyright permissions from her to do so. You could do a quick *Google* search: "Leanne Beetham" and "elephant painting" or "donkey painting."

What is your favorite leisure/ recreation activity? It could be anything that you enjoy doing. It could be skateboarding, surfing, running, or painting as discussed above. You don't have to be the best in the world at the activity. You could persistently work towards becoming the best that you can be at a given activity. I enjoy writing during my leisure time. I'm not the greatest author in the world, but I continue improving my skill by writing when I have free time to do so.

Freedom

Freedom is the basic concept of leisure. Geoffrey Godby is one of the greatest scholars in the field of leisure and recreation. Today, Godby is a Professor Emeritus at Penn State University. He is the author of several texts in the field of leisure and recreation.

I've found Godby's (1985) definition of "leisure" that is featured in his book *Leisure in Your Life* to be the best:

Leisure is:

"Living in relative freedom from the external compulsive forces of one's culture and physical environment so as to be able to act from internally compelling love in ways which are personally pleasing, intuitively worthwhile, and provide a basis for faith. (p. 9)."

Here is my understanding of Godby's (1985) definition. Freedom has two parts according to Godby. These include "freedom from" and "freedom to."

Freedom "from" refers to work, activities of daily living, chores, or other tasks that a person must fulfill. These are things that a person must do from time to time. We've all got responsibilities. You may have a job, or babies to care for, or certain things that must be done. That is life. We've all got these things to do.

Freedom "to" refers to the choice to decide what a person wants to do when she (or he) is not engaged in work or other activities. This freedom of choice allows the individual to excel and become the best that she (or he) can be. It allows for the individual to do something that she loves. It is being involved in something worthwhile and meaningful.

Freedom to do what you love becomes so meaningful that a person is compelled to do it. This could include a pianist who loves to play the piano. This could be the athlete's love for the game. It could be a quilters need to quilt because it frees her soul.

A person has free choice to engage in activities that she (or he) feels passionate about doing. It helps a person to become self-aware. She (or he) learns what she enjoys through trying. She sees what she can accomplish. It is a way for becoming proud. The individual says, "Hey, look what I can do?" It is living to one's fullest ability.

Recreation improves your abilities

Recreation gives a person a chance to re-create their life. It allows a person to have self-discovery. A person learns what she (or he) likes and what she wants to do through recreation. It makes learning easier because of the element of "free choice." People learn more when they "want to learn" and when they enjoy learning.

It has been my personal experience that school focuses on forcing kids to learn. Schools are pressured to teach kids. Often times, children do not have any choice about what they learn or how the lessons are instructed. I've heard high school teens say that they can't wait to get out of school. Why? They want to begin "real" learning that can't be taught in a classroom.

Again, based on my experiences, education doesn't allow for people to discover their real talents. Education is based on teaching all children the same basic courses. Each child gets the same curriculum despite interests and talents. It focuses on the basics of reading, writing, and analyzing. These are wonderful skills to have. School does a good job at teaching these basic skills. School does not, however, allow for a child to have creative learning experiences, which are best achieved through her (or his) leisure experiences. I think children should have more choice and control over the courses they're taking and the way lessons are taught. Having more freedom makes it more interesting. People don't like to be forced to read a book. They want to select a book they want to read. I imagine they'll learn better from a book they enjoy, too.

Ken Robinson in his (2009) book, *The Element: How Finding Your Passion Changes Everything* argues that our current education system is not good enough. He says that our complete education system needs to be revamped because the future is changing. Robinson points out that children today will retire in the year 2070. We can't imagine what their future will hold. One thing is certain. It will require for people to have new skills. It will require "creativity and independent thinking." Robinson argues that our schools are not preparing children to learn these things.

My solution: I think schools should be designed to give children a block of leisure learning. This isn't recess, but a time for self-development and personal growth. It's a time when the child can explore her (or his) own interests and to be more creative. I'm willing to bet that many children would be attracted to creating websites and other computer related programs. However, it could be anything creative that requires independent thinking and trial experiences.

Today, adults in their 50s may feel suave because they can check email and use a computer. Children and teens are programming these computers and doing things that are unimaginable without a college degree in computers. They love it and have passion for it. School isn't necessarily teaching them how to use technology. Children are downloading music, creating *Youtube* videos, and movies, and doing all kinds of things during their leisure time. They have real knowledge that has come from using their recreation pursuits.

Recreation is a form of re-creating oneself. Anytime a person does recreation activities she (or he) is creating a newer self. She is building on her previous talents and getting better. Using computers and technology is an intellectual type of activity. It isn't the only type of leisure and recreation.

Leisure domains

There are several domains for leisure activities. These include: physical, social, intellectual, spiritual, creativity, and relaxation.

Here is a basic overview of each of these domains:

- Physical: This includes anything where a person engages in physical activity. This could consist of: walking, jogging, running, exercising, or sports.

- Social: This includes activities that a person does with other people. These could include: family picnic, night out with friends, or reunions

- Intellectual: These activities require mental stimulation. This could include reading a book, visiting a museum, attending a seminar, or completing a crossword puzzle.

- Spiritual: This is where a person participates in activities related to their belief and faith. It could include: prayer, church, and religious services.

- Creativity: These activities allow for a person to express herself (or himself). This could include: painting, drawing, song-writing, or creating music.

- Relaxation: These activities allow for a person to feel calm and collect. It could include: yoga, meditation, taking a bath, reading, or listening to calming music.

Leisure activities can consist of more than one domain. An activity often overlaps with other domains. Football is an example. It requires for a person to be physically active. A person must run, pass the ball, and tackle the other player. Football is also a social activity. The player is on a team with other people. There is a coach. Fans come to watch the games. There are cheerleaders present. It is very social as well as physical. The game is also intellectual. The player must think ahead and memorize different plays. Some people may find participating in football to be relaxing.

Play some games

Games are great ways to have fun. It gives you the opportunity to be great at something. Games could include: table tennis, pool, cards, dominoes, and even video games.

Games could include fitness activities. You could take up martial arts, snowboarding, swimming, wakeboarding, weight training, horseback riding, dancing, or badminton.

Have a family fun night. This is one night a week where the family plays games like *Scrabble, Uno, Phase 10, Monopoly,* and other games. Focus on having a good time and being with family opposed to winning.

No family – no problem. Create a group to play games. My grandparents got together to play *Bridge* and other card games with friends from their church once a week. My brother and his friends get together to play *Star Wars* and *Lord of the Ring* role-play games. I got together with a group of my friends during college for "game night." We'd always play *Clue*, order pizza, and watch a movie.

A game night is about having fun with friends. It isn't about winning. It doesn't matter who wins. There is a (2008) movie, called, *21*, that shows that it isn't about winning in one scene. The movie is about the game of "Blackjack." A girl in the movie, Jill Taylor is telling Ben Campbell about playing blackjack with her father as a child. Jill says, "If I won, my dad took me out for ice cream." Ben asked, "And if you lost?" Jill replied, "He still took me out for ice cream." It wasn't about winning; it was about quality time between Jill and her father. You should have the same approach when having a game night with family or friends.

Start a hobby

You could start a collection. There are millions of leisure activities that you could get involved with if you're not already doing something. It will give you an excellent opportunity to work towards greatness. Become the best at your hobby or leisure interest.

Entertainment

Entertainment can add a little excitement to your life. Where are some places in your local community that you could visit for entertainment? You could go to the movies, see a play, and attend local events, fairs, and shows. Even if you don't have a friend or partner to do things with, go anyway. Chances are you'll still have a good time and possibly meet someone else who didn't have anyone to go with. Going alone allows you to meet new people and create new healthy relationships.

Why participate in leisure activities?

Satisfaction in life could be the best part for participating in leisure and recreation activities. You could find your life to be more meaningful if you've started a hobby or new leisure pursuit that you're passionate about. You'll have a more interesting life.

A person who sits at home all the time watching television and re-runs is not going to have anything interesting to happen. How does a person start having a more interesting life? She participates in leisure activities. She starts doing something. She could volunteer for an organization that she loves. She could start a new hobby. She could start spending time with her friends. She could eat at new places or try new things. Life will become better and more interesting. Life will become greater.

Health improves as a result of participating in leisure activities. Scientific research has shown that people who actively participate in leisure activities have better coping skills. They can handle life stressors better than those people who do not participate in leisure. As a result of better coping, the person has better immune system and physical health. You could benefit from leisure and recreation in many ways.

The Hidden Secret Revealed in Chapter 8:

Start participating in activities that you are passionate about doing because you're more likely to become great at things you enjoy.

*** Upcoming Attraction ***

Sometimes, following your passion isn't enough to become great. A little something extra is needed. Continuing reading the next chapter to discover the best way to do anything you've ever dreamed about.

Chapter 8 References

411 Magazine (Producers). *The best of 411 video magazine volume 2* [Motion picture]. United States: 411 Productions.

Berk, S., Bundschuh, R., & Hamilton, B. (2006). *Soul Surfer: A True Story of Faith, Family, and Fighting to Get Back on the Board.* MTV.

Godbey, G. (1985) Leisure in your life. (2nd edition). State College, PA: Venture Publishing.

Luketic, R. (Director), & Steinfield P. (screenplay writer), & Loeb A. (screenplay writer). Mezrich, B. (author). *21* [Motion picture]. United States: Columbia Pictures, Relativity Media, Tigger Street Productions, Michael De Luca Productions, & GH Three.

Robinson, K. (2009). *The Element: How Finding Your Passion Changes Everything*. New York: Viking Adult.

Wikipedia.com (n.d.) *Shea Cowart*. Retrieved April 23, 2009, from: http://en.wikipedia.org/wiki/Shea_Cowart

Chapter 9

Here's The Best Way to Become Great, Get a Job, or Do Anything

> It is how we handle ourselves in our relationships that determine how well we do once we are in a given job.
>
> **- Daniel Goleman**

Social Support

Networks of people can help you to accomplish many great things in life. They can help you to become great. The more people you know the higher your social support will be. These people can include: family, friends, acquaintances, people from work, and people from social groups that you belong to. It is important because we are social beings. Humans need other people. "No woman (or man) is an island," is a popular quote that means a person can't do everything herself (or himself). People need other people in life.

Having people to help you could cause you to have positive feelings. Just knowing that you've got people who can help you gives you a sense of support. You could turn to your support network when you're sad and simply need a shoulder to cry on. You could turn to a friend when you need to vent. You could turn to a friend when you want someone to go out and have fun. You could turn to a friend to borrow money or get a ride or to celebrate a special occasion.

Friends can support you in many ways. More friends mean having more support. There is one downside to having a lot of friends. It could take a toll on you. In return, you'll provide support to your friends from time to time. If you've got 100 real close friends then it could become draining. It would require time, money, attention, and other things. A small clique could be easier to handle. You'll know what social network would be best for you. Some people are more introverted (like me). I get energy from having alone time. Other people are more extraverted. They get energy from being around people. You'll know if you're an introvert or extravert if you've taken the Keirsey's personality test (This was discussed in chapter 1). The key point here is to have a network of friends that you feel comfortable with having.

Who do you know?

Carrie Phillips Pettry Napier was my grandmother (on my father's side). She helped me to get a job when I was a teenager. Carrie and her husband Alex Napier (the only grandfather who I knew) loved to eat at *Chick-fil-A*. For those people outside of the southeastern United States, *Chick-fil-A* is a restaurant that serves chicken sandwiches and chicken nuggets. They're primarily located in the malls.

Carrie knew the owner of the Beckley/ Crossroads Mall, *Chick-fil-A*, Mr. Joe Clark. She tracked him down and cornered him in the mall. She said, "Mr. Clark, you need to hire my grandson, Danny Pettry." She spoke some good, kind words about me. I got an interview within days and I got the job. I can say that it was my grandmother who got me this job. I can say that I, myself, kept the job. I did my best to work hard there. Hard-work is one of my personal values. I helped to get my brother (Jimmy) and sister (Carrie) jobs there, too. Many of my best friends worked there, too. Mr. Joe Clark had a system. He asked us to sign our names at the bottom of an application for a person who we recommend that would be a good fit for *Chick-fil-A*. At least ten employees had signed the bottom of Jimmy and Carrie's employment applications. We recommended our good friends. Knowing people in the right places can help a person to get a job or other things. Of course, you don't need me to give you this advice. You've probably heard the motto, "It isn't what you know, but who you know."

It's a small world

Six degrees is the number that separates a person from any other person in the world. It is based on social psychologist, Stanley Milgram's experiment on connections in the 1960s. Malcom Gladwell, in his (2002) book, *The Tipping Point: How Little Things Can Make a Big Difference*, describes Milgram's experiment. Milgram sent a package to 160 random people in Omaha, Nebraska. Each of these 160 people were instructed to mail the package to someone they knew personally who might be able to get the package to a stockbroker in Boston. On average, it took about five or six people to get it from Omaha to Boston, hence the "six degrees concept."

Here is an example, I, Danny Pettry, am only six degrees (or less) from Zlata Filipović, author of *Zlata's Diary*. She is on my personal list of people who I want to meet someday. I don't know anyone who knows Zlata, but I know someone who knows someone who knows her. Someone reading this book may introduce me to her.

Here is another example: I've never met President Barack Obama myself, but I am three degrees away from him. My grandmother, Donna Keesee (who passed away July 6, 2005 at the age of

84) knew U.S. Senator Robert C. Byrd from her youth in southern West Virginia. My grandmother kept in touch with Senator Byrd through letters for many years. Today, Robert Byrd (the longest serving Senator in history) works closely with President Barack Obama. Both Senator Robert Byrd and President Barack Obama discuss their first meeting on Capitol Hill in their books respectively, *Robert C. Byrd: Child of the Appalachian Coal Fields* and *The Audacity of Hope: Thoughts on Reclaiming the American Dream* by Barack Obama. Senator Robert Byrd gave a set of the *Senate Histories* to Barack Obama and signed it during their meeting.

People may be less than six degrees of each other today. The world has become a lot smaller and closer. This concept has been presented in Thomas Friedman's (2005) book, *The World is Flat: A Brief History of the 21st Century*. Friedman argues that Netscape and the Internet has "flattened" the world and helped to bring people together from around the world. Here is an example: an elementary school student in Seattle, Washington could easily communicate with an elementary student in Columbus, Ohio, Tokyo, Japan, Berlin, Germany, or anyone in the world. They can do this with instant message chatting online and webcams.

You're only a few people away from anyone in the world. You know someone who knows someone who knows someone. Remember that knowing people can help you to become great.

Barack Obama is the 44th President of the United States of America. He'll always be known as our nation's first President of African heritage. He is also the first president to use online social networks in his process to becoming president. Obama had a team to operate a *myspace* page for him. I read his book, *Dreams from My Father: A Story of Race and Inheritance.* I enjoyed his book and did a Google searched on Obama online. I discovered his *myspace* page and added him as a friend in 2007.

Obama was using technology early in the game to become president. I'd argue that *myspace* (an online social network site) helped to get Obama elected.

You can add me [Danny Pettry] as a friend on several online social networks. I have a myspace, facebook, blogspot, linkedin, youtube, and twitter page. You can get my e-newsletter, too.

Danny Pettry on the Internet

Go to this link to add me as a friend or to follow me on my online social networks. I'd love to meet you.

www.hiddensecretwisdom.com/networks

I receive a lot of praise from people through *myspace*. Recreational therapists post comments on my *myspace* page telling me that I've helped them to connect with others to find the right job, get a resource, or meet a professional who is an expert working with a certain age group or population. I feel great satisfaction from helping others.

My good friend from high school, Stef, had to give away her dog. She posted a bulletin on her *myspace* asking if anyone was looking for a dog. I simply copied her bulletin and sent it to the friends on my *myspace* list.

About a week later, Stef sent me this email:

Hey,

Thank you Danny!

Kelli messaged me about her coworker that may be interested [in the dog]. After multiple emails and one phone call, her friend took my dog. Yesterday I met her in Charleston [West Virginia].

Without you reposting my bulletin this would not have been possible.

Thank you again.

I owe you one! :)

Stef

I used my social connections to help Stef to connect with a person she may have never met on her own. I was especially worried because I didn't want the pooch to end up at the dog pound or possibly put to sleep. Knowing people can help you to achieve many great things, too. You could find a home for a pet or find yourself the right pet. You could find a job or find the right person for a job, if you use social networks.

Using connections

Heather Wyman is a creative arts therapist in New Jersey. She is a good friend of mine who I met online through *myspace*. I think she is very inspiring.

Heather is the creative operator of the *6 Degrees to Make a Difference myspace* page. She created this network because many kids who come to her hospital develop a "victim mentality." A person with this type of mindset blames other people for their own problems. An example is if a kid is physically aggressive (biting, kicking, and hurting others) the kid may go to a hospital or treatment center. Opposed to taking responsibility the kid blames parents or the hospital staff for being at a hospital. The child could be a "true victim" if she (or he) has suffered abuse. It becomes a problem when the child continues to blame the world for all of her (or his) problems.

Heather teaches children that they have control of their life. She introduces her kids to other people in the world through *6 Degrees to Make a Difference*. It includes children with cancer, those who have lost parents due to war, and many others. People can network with others across the world with similar situations and experiences. Heather wants to make a difference in the world and she has over 3,000 friends on her *myspace* group. She has a special "Cause of the Week," each week to promote a charity or service.

Check out Heather's *6 Degrees to Make a Difference*, here:

---

www.myspace.com/6degreesnj

Live with people

Happiness is the result of living with other people. Of course, you may be thinking, "yeah right, I hate living with others. We fight a lot." Yes, people do fight from time to time. People with good healthy relationships will work through their disagreements. Having a supportive family can cause a person to feel happy. A family could offer you support when you need it. Studies show that people who live alone are more likely to have a shorter lifespan compared to those people who live with others. Research studies link people who are isolated with a high rate of early death. Some people argue that social isolation is as dangerous as smoking cigarettes. It is not healthy for a person.

Imagine this situation: If a person lives alone and she chokes on dinner one night, who'll ever know? She could die right then and there. If she lives with others, it is more likely that someone will find her and use the heimlich maneuver to save her life. She'll most likely be eating with others during the same time, too. It is far better to live with other people than to be isolated.

People skills

Social Intelligence is discussed by Daniel Goleman in his (2007) book with the same name. Goleman argues that having high social and emotional intelligence is far greater predictor of success compared to having a high I.Q.

Social Intelligence, according to Goleman is having an awareness of social skills. It is the ability to relate and talk to other people. This includes having interpersonal skills, empathy for others, having clarity, and understanding social situations.

Having a high I.Q. is a good thing, but having social skills is a must. Here is an example that I learned from Goleman. Imagine a super smart scientist. He's wearing a lab coat. He talks to you in technical terms. You don't understand his scientific jargon. You're aware that the scientist is intelligent, but he can't get the point across in simple terms. You'll want to ask: will you just speak to me in English, please?

Now, let's imagine a second scientist. This guy has "people skills." He is smart, but he also knows how to communicate with people. He explains things to you in simple, clear terms that you understand. You see the big picture. This person is more likely to make more friends, get promoted, and become the boss.

Ronald Reagan (40th President of the United States) was known as the "great communicator." He was an excellent orator who could speak in terms that people understood. Barack Obama (44th

President of the United States) is also a great communicator. He talks smooth and eloquently. He's easy to understand. People can listen to him and know what he's talking about.

You've got to have good communication skills if you want to become successful. *Toast Masters International* is a non-profit organization that can help you to develop public speaking and leadership skills by giving speeches and receiving feedback.

Bella vs. David in I.Q.

I've known a girl since high school who I'll call, "Bella" to protect her real identity. Bella was kind, smart, and very shy. She was ranked in the top ten of her class of about 400 students when she graduated.

"David" is another guy who I've known for quite some time. David ranked 150 out of nearly 400 students in the same class.

Bella and David had both taken the ACT exam on the same day. A person must take this exam before being accepted to a college. Bella and David both anxiously awaited their test scores. Bella knew she would do well. She was always the first one to complete assignments in class and she would always have a 100%. Some teachers even allowed her to grade other student's papers because she was first to finish and always had excellent scores. [I don't agree with having a student grade papers, but that is a different story that won't be told here.]

Finally, their ACT scores arrived. The ACT test scores range from 1 (low) to 36 (high). David earned a "15." Colleges in West Virginia required at least an 18 to be accepted in 1998. They may have raised the bar to a score of at least "21" now. Bella, in a playful way, teased and laughed that she had twice David's score, plus two. She earned a "32." David had to take basic courses at the local college that didn't count towards a degree to make up for his "15."

Bella was awarded a full scholarship to a major university in our state, West Virginia. They even gave her a laptop. It paid for everything, including: room, board, college tuition, her text books, and it even gave her an allowance for free spending each semester.

Test scores are important, or at least, that is what we're taught in school and in life. However, these scores might not be as important as you think. People value these high scores as an indicator for who will be successful in college.

Here is an important question to ask: Who becomes a success in life? Is it the smartest person or is it a person with good interpersonal skills and self-awareness? I'd argue it is probably a person who is smart and self-aware, but also has super social skills.

Let's reexamine the real life example that I know: Bella "with a 32" and David "with a 15." Who do you think will become more successful in college based on their test scores alone? Naturally, you'd think Bella because she was 4 points shy of having a perfect score.

Bella had a hard time adjusting to college and became very depressed. She was shy and didn't have many friends to reach out to when in need. Bella fell into the wrong peer group during college. She started drinking, which wasn't the best combination with her depression and lack of a positive social support network. As a result, she didn't do well in college.

Bella also lacked self-awareness. She didn't know what she really wanted to do in life. She could have benefited from reading chapter one in this book to discover who she is and what she wants in life. She didn't have any motivation to do well in college.

Bella failed her first semester in college and was put on probation. She had to make a certain grade point average the second semester or she'd lose her scholarship. She lost it. She ended up moving back home with her mother and began working as a grocery clerk. She worked at the grocery store for a decade. As a reminder, there isn't anything wrong with this type of work. I'm glad she has a job. However, Bella could have been anything she wanted to be. She could have been a doctor, lawyer, nurse, or anything. She was smart enough to do it.

Bella had a higher ACT score than David. Shouldn't she have been more successful in college? One would think so. Research supported by Daniel

Goleman in his (2007) book, *Social Intelligence* says otherwise.

David, on the other hand completed his basic courses at a local college that didn't count towards hid degree. He was able to transfer to a more prestigious university in the state after proving he could handle college courses for one-year. David completed an undergraduate degree and then went on to pursue a graduate degree at an out-of-state university. Today, David works as a counselor. David was different because he had social interaction skills, more friends, and he knew what he wanted in life. David went to college with a goal in mind. He knew early in the game that he wanted to be a counselor and he was dedicated.

How to develop a social network

Social activities and clubs are great ways to build a social support network. Start today by joining a club or organization. Join one that you're interested in being a member.

- If you've always wanted to get in shape and you have a little spiritual side, then consider yoga.

- If you've always wanted to learn self-defense, then consider Tae Kwon Do.

- If you've always loved books, join a book club.

- Joining a club could be a great way to make new friends with people who enjoy doing the same thing you enjoy.

- Volunteer. This is a great way to meet people and make new friends. There are many places you could volunteer. Consider the V.A. hospital, a nursing home, or an after school programs for children. Do you have a talent or special gift? If so, volunteer to teach others. This will get you out there. It will help you to be more active and social. You'll meet people and build a network of new friends.

Do more activities. Get out and do things. Do anything. Go to an event, fair, seminar, or social activity. Read your newspaper's section on local events. It'll feature many free things.

Read *How to Win Friends and Influence People*

A review of Dale Carnegie's (1936)
How to Win Friends and Influence People

Dale Carnegie is the "grandfather" of people skills. He had written, the classic (1936) book, *How to Win Friends and Influence People,* which practically became a bestseller overnight. His book is one of my personal all-time favorites. It was the first full book that I had read and I've been reading books every since then. I thought this book was absolutely amazing even if it was published 44 years before I was born. It is a book that all people should read.

What are some of the secrets to winning friends and influencing people? Carnegie suggests:

- Smile at other people,
- Take an interest in others,
- Speak well of other people, and
- Make other people feel important.

Think of a person who doesn't use these principles. This is a person who never smiles and never has anything kind to say. He doesn't care what you have to say or anything about you. He never fully listens and often interrupts you to talk about his own interests. His attitude is awful. Just seeing this person makes you want to walk the other way. Don't let this person be you. Be the exception. Be the person that everyone likes. How? Be likeable.

I am very fortunate to have learned these people skills directly from my parents. My mother and father have good people skills. The book was like reinforcement, a reminder, or a wake-up call. It was as if I had always known these techniques, but the book brought them to my attention.

People said that my grandmother, Carrie Pettry Napier never knew a stranger. She was always smiling. She always had kind words to say about people and she made friends everywhere. My father has the same skill. He is always smiling. I've never heard anyone say a negative word about him.

Read Carnegie's book and apply what he teaches to your own life.

Read *The 5 Love Languages*

A Review of Gary Chapman's (1995)
*The 5 Love Languages: How to Express Heartfelt
Commitment to Your Mate*

I first discovered Gary Chapman's (1995)
The 5 Love Languages as a college student at
Marshall University. We had monthly classes in the
dorms. They had a nice bribe to get residents to
attend. They always offered free pizza, chips and
cola. Sometimes, I'd go to these sessions with some
of the guys from the dorm. Different speakers
would present on different topics.

It was around Valentine's Day, and a teacher
from Marshall University's Campus Crusaders for
Christ (CCC) presented on the meaning of real love.
This was the only session from the dorm classes I
remember really being interested in learning about.
The presenter recommended Gary Chapman's *The
Five Love Languages* among other books. I
immediately went to Borders Bookstore at the
Huntington Mall the next day to buy the book.

People, networks, friendships, groups, and
relationships are key ingredients to becoming
successful and great in life. Chapman presents some
of the best techniques I've ever heard on expressing
love and concern for others in his (1995) book.
Chapman's techniques are not just for romantic love
either. You could use his five love languages to
show anyone you care.

Chapman (1995) explains these five ways to
express love that are shown on the next page:

- Using your words
- Giving gifts
- Spending quality time
- Doing a favor or chore
- Using physical touch

The Hidden Secret Revealed in Chapter 9:

Develop people skills. Know no stranger.
Create a strong social support network.

*** Upcoming Attraction ***

Doing kind deeds can help you increase your people skills. Continue reading to the next chapter to learn how you can become a do-gooder in order to become great and successful.

<u>Chapter 9 References</u>

Carnegie, D. (1998). *How to Win Friends & Influence People*. New York: Pocket.

Chapman, G. (1995). *The Five Love Languages: How to Express Heartfelt Commitment to Your Mate*. hyderabad: Northfield Publishing.

Friedman, T. L. (2006). *The World Is Flat: A Brief History of the Twenty-first Century*. New York: Farrar. Straus And Giroux.

Gladwell, M. (2002). *The Tipping Point: How Little Things Can Make a Big Difference*. New York: Back Bay Books.

Goleman, D. (2007). *Social Intelligence: The New Science of Human Relationships*. United States and Canada: Bantam.

Chapter 10

Why Do-Gooders are More Likely to Become Great and Successful

"How wonderful it is that nobody need wait a single moment before starting to improve the world."

- Anne Frank

One of the greatest do-gooders

Oskar Schindler (b. 1908 d. 1974) was one of the greatest helpers in the world. He was born in Austria – Hungary and was raised Catholic. His first goal as a young adult was to make money. He wanted to become wealthy. This was during World War II. Schindler bought a factory in Poland. He hired people who were Jewish as cheap labor. This was during the Holocaust when Hitler's Nazi party was murdering people who were Jewish.

Mr. Schindler had a change of heart during this time. He was no longer running a factory just to make money. He realized what the Nazi party was doing. His work changed to save the people who worked at his factory. He'd hire people who were unskilled or had disabilities. Schindler would argue with the German police that his workers were needed (despite many being unskilled or disabled.) As a result, Schindler saved them from deportation to concentration camps, which meant certain death. Schindler knew the concentration camps were primarily designed to kill people who were Jewish. He saved the lives of thousands of people.

Schindler helped to transport children who were Jewish to live with nuns to save their lives. He'd claim the orphans were "Christians" in order to save them from certain death by the Nazis.

Schindler could have been killed by the Nazi party for saving a person who was Jewish. This makes him outstanding. He did the right thing. He did something great.

Schindler acquired another factory that made missiles and other weapons for the Nazis during WWII. Schindler made one thing certain. He didn't want a single weapon to be produced at the factory while he was in charge of it. He didn't want the Nazi party to have more things they could use to hurt people.

Wealth was once plentiful for Schindler. Overtime, his wealth depleted because he ran factories to save people. Schindler would offer bribes to Nazi officers in order to save people at his factory. Schindler died at the age of 66. He was awarded the *Yad Vashem*. It's an award for non-Jewish people who risked their lives to save people who are Jewish during the Holocaust.

I highly recommend that you watch Steven Spielberg's (1993) movie, *Schindler's List*, which is based on Schindler saving people.

You should do good deeds, too

Earth is our home. All humans must live on this blue planet together. It is like a giant house and humans are like a big family. Are we a happy family or are we an unhappy family? Are we getting-along with each other or are we not-getting-along? Is our overall family functional or dysfunctional? Do you want to live in a good world or a not-so-good world? No matter how you answer these questions, the key is to take care of your home (our whole world). Take care of where you live and reach out to others, help them live and grow.

Do good deeds in the world because it is the right thing to do. We've all got to live together so my suggestion is to make it a happy, peaceful home. We can do this by being kind towards other people. It doesn't matter where a person lives. You can be nice to other people regardless if they're from China, Mexico, Japan, England, Africa, or anywhere else in the world. Think about the children, the elderly, and the sick in places like Iraq, Iran, or anywhere else in the world. If every single U.S. citizen did one kind deed to help a person in another place then we'd be sure to make many new friends in the world. The entire world could become a better, more peaceful and friendly place for all of us to live.

Good is at the heart of all people. This is the basic concept behind humanistic psychology. It is the belief that deep down, all people are good, have good intentions, and strive to do better. I think that Anne Frank best describes the humanistic approach, in her book, *Anne Frank's Diary*. Anne was a victim of the holocaust. She died in a concentration camp weeks before it was liberated. She had kept a detailed diary about her life and her experiences hiding in an attic from the Nazi party. Here is what Anne had to say:

> "I still believe, in spite of everything,
> that people are truly good at heart."
>
> **Anne Frank**

Humanistic psychology approach leaves the control in the hands of a person. It is unlike the behaviorist approach (primarily developed by B. F. Skinner). Behaviorists attempt to control and manipulate people through the use of punishments and rewards. Punishment often appears as a "cruel and unusual" approach to manipulating people into change. Behaviorist psychologists have moved away from punishments, including: spankings, whippings, etc. Today, the behaviorist psychologist attempts to seduce and persuade people through the use of rewards, which are not effective at producing long-term change. The new behavior stops once the reward is lessened.

Real, lasting change must be self-directed and internal. A person doesn't need to be externally rewarded to do good deeds. Schindler was a good example. He lost money as a result of helping. He wasn't doing good deeds to profit. He did it for a greater reason, something internal.

Real change must be self-directed. This is a key to the humanistic approach. Rewards are external motivators. They're used to control a person and they imply that a person can't be self-directed to make the right choice. Here is an excellent example of how rewards are not effective:

Malcom Gladwell in his (2008) book, *Outliers: The Story of Success*, makes an argument that external rewards are not the strongest motivator for work. Here's the question Gladwell asks: Would you rather have a job making $100,000 a year working as a toll booth operator. Remember, this job would have the same routine each day that could become boring. Or would you rather settle for a $75,000 year job as a creative architect that allows you to have free choice over where your office is and how you design structures. Which would you choose? Most people would choose the architect position unless they were desperate for money. Why? Because it offers a chance for self-direction and free will. An external motivator like $100,000 doesn't change a person. It is her (or his) internal motivation that produces change. A person may be influenced by the money to do something, but that doesn't mean her (or his) heart is fully dedicated to doing it.

Do something good for a friend, today

Strong friendships are the key to becoming great. A person with many friends has achieved a great accomplishment. The person without any friends will suffer greatly in life. That person won't have support to get thing things she (or he) needs in life. Do one kind thing for each of your friends today. Think back to the last chapter on social support. Remember Gary Chapman's *5 Love Languages*? Do some of these things for your friends.

Unconsciously people will want to return the favor. Naturally, you shouldn't do good deeds in an attempt to manipulate people into doing something for you. This would be inauthentic. Hidden agendas like this aren't good.

It's fairly easy to do or be good for a friend. It isn't as easy to do-good for an enemy.

Do something good for an enemy, today, too

Enemies are people, too. They have needs and wants just like we do. But the question remains, why does an enemy treat us in not-so-nice ways? Why do they do the things they do? It was just written earlier in this chapter that all people do good, right?

There are two reasons why a person may not do good things.

- "When they're bad it's because they're coping with some need beyond their control," according to Maslow. Here is an example: if a person is rude to you in public - it probably has nothing to do with you. They could be dealing with something that you couldn't even imagine. They're not intentionally seeking to do you wrong. They're just dealing with strong negative emotions. This isn't an excuse for their behavior, however. But it isn't anything personal.

- A second reason why people do not-so-good things to us is because they think they're *doing good*. They don't believe it is bad. Dr. Rick Brinkman and Dr. Rick Kirschner in their (2003) book, *Dealing with People You Can't Stand: How to Bring Out the Best in People at Their Worst* argue that all people have "good intentions." They may be doing something that you can't stand, but the other person is only doing it because she (or he) thinks that it is the right thing to do.

Having an understanding of the above two principles could help you to become more understanding of why others may be not-so-nice. They're either dealing with something stressful or they're doing it because they think they're doing the right thing.

Go ahead and do something nice for someone who you don't get along with very well. This will be the start at making change. It will be the start of something great.

Volunteer

Volunteering is the basis for this chapter. Why are do-gooders more likely to be successful? Good feelings usually come from volunteering. People who are happy are more likely to be successful. You may discover that you like the way you feel about yourself when you do wonderful things for other people.

You could discover your life mission or purpose doing good deeds. This would give you something to aim at. It would be something to achieve.

I discovered my passion from volunteering. In 1999, I had to complete a 40-hour week of volunteer/ observation work before I could be accepted into any health degree program at Mountain State University (former Beckley College). I did mine at *HealthSouth Rehabilitation Hospital* of Huntington, West Virginia. At *HealthSouth,* I discovered my passion and what I wanted to do in life.

Tracy Meadows-Forrest (my cousin) was a physical therapist at *HealthSouth Rehab*. Her husband, Adam Forrest was the director of occupational therapy services. I was a young 19-year-old who was undecided about what I wanted to do with my life. I got to watch Adam and Tracy help people. It wasn't until my second day of volunteer work that I discovered what I wanted to do with my life, which was to become a recreational therapist.

People in the hospital were sick. Many of them were in pain. They were away from their homes. Many of the people were sad.

Laughter and music came from a back room. My curiosity led me to go back there and check things out. This is where I discovered recreational therapy. Mark, the recreational therapist and a Marshall University recreational therapy intern, Marci Osborne were leading an arts & craft group activity for the patients. They had music playing. The room was filled with crafts and plants. It was colorful and enjoyable. I knew I had to get involved in this. Mark and Marci were using craft projects to help get patients to build stamina and to use their arms in adaptive ways. The patients were having fun doing therapy. They were having a better quality of life that they would not have had without the recreational therapy program at *HealthSouth*. I spent the rest of the week with Mark and Marci learning all I could about what it takes to become a recreational therapist and learning how I could help others to have a better quality of life.

The recreational therapy program at *HealthSouth* included: creative arts and crafts, stress management, relaxation training, and, social activities including: cook-outs, gardening, and community reintegration outings. The stress management and relaxation sessions were my favorite. Mark would lead a discussion on different topics for the patients. It was held on the back patio or by the plants that the patients had planted when the weather was appropriate. This session allowed patients to learn ways to cope, to express their feelings, and to have opportunity for social interaction and relaxation. Calming music would be played during the last five to ten minutes. I realized during this week that I wanted to be a therapist like Mark and Marci. I wanted to become a recreational therapist, too.

Helping became my passion right then and there. I transported patients to and from groups by pushing their wheelchairs. I'd run and get a coffee for a patient in group. Mark and Marci would warn me if a patient had a special diet. I'd help serve patients during the cook-out. I'd talk and listen to patients. It made me feel good.

Here is a task for you. Go out and volunteer. Do anything. It could be something you love to do. You could read to children. You could volunteer at the Veteran's Hospital or a nursing home. Help at the homeless shelter. Donate blood. Recycle. Plant a tree. I recommend a fruit tree because it will offer food one day. Teach skills that you know to people for free. You could participate in a community project. You could find yourself feeling a lot better.

You could discover your real passion in life through volunteering. I did.

Two ways to make a difference

Time is quality. It requires you to be there. If you were to give one hour a week to doing good then you'd do 52 hours of good work in one year. You would do 520 hours of good work in ten years. That is a lot of time. Imagine if 1,000 people did one hour of volunteer work or good deeds a week. That would be 52,000 hours of good work in one year alone. It would make the world a better place. People would be better off because of your great actions. It would make you a better person. You'd develop your skills and abilities. You'd be using your time more productive opposed to sitting around watching television. The world needs people like you to make a difference. Using your time will also give you a more interesting life. You'll have stories to share because of all the wonderful and interesting experiences.

Money is a second way you could make the world better. Start giving today. Many people say that they'll give when they have it. They say, "I'll give it when I make 100,000 or a million dollars," but they don't. You must start now. If you don't do it now then you surely won't later. It is like the "Free Doughnuts Tomorrow" sign. Everyone gets excited because it reads: FREE, but there is a catch. Everyday the sign still reads: *Tomorrow.* It is just words. It is not real. Tomorrow never comes. My point is that you've got to start today. Don't say you'll start tomorrow. Henry Ford said that a person can't build a reputation on what he says he's going to do. Basically, words are cheap. They don't mean anything. Action does. Money does. Use your money in constructive ways.

I admire the *Chicken Soup Series* by Jack Canfield and Mark Victor Hansen. Each book has a charity. It gives a portion of the profits to a service. One book raises money to plant fruit trees. Another book raises money for the Red Cross. I'm imitating their greatness with the book you're holding and reading now. Part of the profits from this book goes towards the non-profit charity, *First Book*. For information, go here: http://www.firstbook.org

Give just a little each pay check. If you don't have money, then give of your time. Just give. Great people give. Selfish people don't.

Clean

Help people by giving your stuff away. You've already got things that you could just give away. These are things that you never use. There could be clothes in your closet right now that have been there for years that you've not touched and probably won't. Give these to people in need. Do a major spring cleaning even if it is autumn. Make two stacks: one stack of things to give away and another stack to recycle.

How can you tell if you should keep it? I heard the answer to this on the radio once. A guy on the radio said that he had moved from Cincinnati, Ohio to Huntington, West Virginia or vice versa 10 years ago. He still had boxes that he hadn't unpacked yet. He started throwing the full boxes away. He said that if he'd gone this long without using its contents in the box then he could go the rest of his life without them. I don't recommend throwing things out without knowing the contents. He does give a good way to determine if you really need it. If you're not opening and using it then you probably don't need it.

I think the purpose in life is to give. It isn't to collect and have the most stuff. We all know that a person can't take these things with her (or him) when she passes away.

I read a lot and I have many of books. I know that I'll never read some books twice, so I just give them away. I give some to the library at the hospital that I work at. I give others to family members. I give some away as contests at my website: www.DannyPettry.Com. I give books to co-workers, family, and friends.

Tim Sanders in his (2003) book, *Love is the Killer App: How to Win Business and Influence Friends* said, "It's hard to beat the gift of a book. It's a great way to show love and add value." Abraham Lincoln (16th President of the United States) said: "The things I want to know are in books; my best friend is a man who'll get me a book I haven't read."

Many used books look new when you give them away as well. It's just a little extra bonus when you give them away. Books can inspire. Books can educate and they can take you places where you've never been. A book could change a person's life. Knowledge is great.

Sponsor a child

Children are people. They have their own basic needs. I believe all children should have food, clothing, shelter, love, education, and their basic human needs met. Children are born into the world without any control of what situation they'll be born into. They may be born into great richness or into poverty. They could be born in the least wealthy nation in the world. No matter where a child is born and lives, you can help her (or him) by being a sponsor. If you can't help financially, consider becoming a "Big Brother or a Big Sister," which is a volunteer to help children. For more information, go to this website for more information:

---

www.bbbs.org

Help the world become a better place. You could sponsor a child in another nation through a service like *Feed the Children*. This is a Christian organization that helps to feed children (as its name implies) and it also provides some other needs for the child. It's really neat because you get a picture of the child and you can write to her (or him). It is really nice to see the benefits of a service like this. A little money each month can do so much for a child in a not-so-wealthy situation. For more information, go to this website:

---

www.feedthechildren.org

Please note that I'm not advocating for Christianity or any religion, nor will I share my personal religious or political beliefs. I am suggesting that you do good deeds. Give back and make the world a better place. Give to people.

The Hidden Secret Revealed in Chapter 10:

Help make this world a better and greater place. Give to people in need. You could discover your passion and mission in life by doing so.

*** Upcoming Attraction ***

Doing good deeds for others can help to make you a greater person. You've also got to take care of yourself. What good would it be if you're not able to carry out your purpose or mission in life because you've not taken care of yourself? Read the upcoming chapter to get motivation and inspiration for living a healthy life. It'll be simple, easy, and fun.

Chapter 10 References

Brinkman, R., & Kirschner, R. (2002). *Dealing with People You Can't Stand: How to Bring Out the Best in People at Their Worst*. New York: McGraw-Hill.

Gladwell, M. (2008). *Outliers: The Story of Success*. Boston: Little, Brown.

Keneally, T. (1994). *Schindler's List*. New York: Simon & Schuster.

"I'm donating my antique clock after
you challenged me to give of my time."

© 2009 Jonny Hawkins

© 2009 by Jonny Hawkins. Reprinted with permission.
All rights reserved.

Chapter 11

A Health and Fitness Program Can Help You to Become Great... Guaranteed!

"Make the most of yourself,
for that is all there is to you.

- Ralph Waldo Emerson

Health and wellness

Self-image is a must if you want to become successful. Always keep a positive attitude toward yourself. If you feel good about yourself you'll project that "feel good" image to other people who you meet. Exercise to keep the outside of your body healthy and watch what you eat to keep your inside body healthy. When you feel good about yourself you'll feel more comfortable and relaxed when you're out in public and around people.

Imagine some of the greatest people in the world. They take care of their body. Athletes like Michael Jordon, Tiger Woods, and Tony Hawk are in shape. Think of people with disabilities. John Comer, Bethany Hamilton, and Shea Cowart are in-shape. I'm not suggesting that you aim for anything unrealistic. Do the best with what you've got.

Take care of your overall body. I've heard kids say, I have good vision and I might never need glasses. A person who lives long enough will probably need glasses at some point in their lives.

The key is to take care of your vision, hearing, and overall health as well. Try to see a dentist twice a year to make sure your teeth are in good shape. Get an eye exam every so often. These are the basics ingredients for maintaining good health and wellness. It will help you to look good and feel good about yourself.

Be presentable if you want to be great. You must look your best. I heard on the radio once that people from my home state of West Virginia are often discriminated against because of their appearance. Unfortunately, many people in the state have poor quality teeth because they lack dental insurance. Big companies want to hire people with beautiful smiles to work their front lines and to promote their products. They'll select a person with better-looking teeth for the job.

Take care of your health and wellness. It is your body. It's the only one you've been given. It is your personal responsibility. There are no other people who are going to do this for you. It is 100% up to you. You've got to do it.

Quality of life will be increased by taking care of your health and wellness. You'll feel better, look better, and have more energy. You'll be able to do many great things with all of this energy. You'll be able to do more things and possibly all the things you've wanted to do. Start taking better care of your health if you're not already doing so. It's vital if you want to become great.

Disclaimer Notice: Talk to your physician before starting a new diet or exercise program to see what is right for you.

Benefits

In marketing, it is said that, people are more likely to buy because of the benefits. I'll remind you of the benefits for exercising here to encourage you to buy into the idea of doing it. Naturally, you'll have better health, more energy, less illness, more flexibility, and a longer, more satisfying life.

Preventive medicine

Physical activity will help prevent many illnesses. Exercise is known for decreasing the risk for heart attacks, strokes, and many other health problems. You'll be able to do more. It strengthens bone structure. Exercise builds strength and endurance. You'll be able to live longer and healthier. This could give you more time on Earth to do great things with your life. You won't be able to do as many good things if you're sick and ill. So, it is vital that you take care of yourself in order to reach your greatest potential.

Use your journal

I was going to title this section, how a woman lost 25 lbs. on the yellow legal pad diet. This diet has two easy parts.

First, keep a food journal. At the top of the page, write the date. Write what you eat on this page. Include everything you had for breakfast, lunch, dinner, and snack. Include anything you drink. Write down a tic-tac or small piece of gum. This will help you to have a better awareness of what you're putting in your body. It is a good record that you can show your physician the next time you have an appointment, too. You could be amazed at what you're actually eating. Knowing that you're going to write it down could help you to curve your eating patterns.

Second, write down a record of your exercises and physical fitness participation. This can be done on one sheet of paper in your journal or on a sheet of yellow legal pad paper. Create three columns. Here are the titles to write at the top of each column: date, activity, and time. Write down each time you do a physical activity. Here is an example, one line could read: March 1st, walked at park, 30 minutes. A second line could read: March 2nd, lifted weights at gym, 20 minutes. A third line could read: March 3rd, rode bike with friends, 45 minutes. Work towards a goal of exercising 30 minutes to one hour every day.

Get a buddy

Support can help you stick to your health and wellness program. You're more likely to stay with it if you have a "buddy system." You can do activities together, like walking, bike riding, yoga, golfing, aerobics, swimming, etc.

Dedication will be the result of a buddy system. It's positive peer pressure. You won't want to be the one to break the cycle. It is easy to give-up when you're doing it alone. It's a little more difficult to give up if you've got a buddy. She'll call you and say, I'm on my way over so we can go to the park as we had planned. Or you could call her and give her the reminder. Having a buddy system will help you keep to your commitment.

Enjoyment will be the result of a buddy system. You'll have more fun. You'll have a friend who'll be doing activities with you. You won't have to go alone. Going alone takes a lot of courage. You might have to fight the embarrassment or fear of going the first time. It's like anything else you do, the more you do it the easier it becomes.

Fun is the key to making exercise enjoyable. You could participate in physical activities that you like to do. This will encourage you do to them more. Simple exercise can seem boring to most people.

There are hundreds of activities that a person could do that require some physical activity. Some of these include: dance, yoga, walking, swimming, jogging, hiking, soccer, and so many more. Do some thinking and decide on something that you'd like to do for fitness. Do these activities at your level. You don't have to be the best at it. In fact, anyone who ever began anything wasn't the best in the world the first time they tired. Just go out and start doing some physical activity. I suppose, *Nike*, the company that makes tennis shoes for sports and fitness activities had it right with their slogan, "just do it."

Team sport

Team sports offer you something different. They require other people. This could help you to be more social. It could help you to make friends and networks. It could help you to stay involved.

Some team sports include: baseball, softball, basketball, soccer, football, or volleyball. You could even participate on a team in tennis or be involved in a bowling league.

Know your limits. Different people at different ages have different skills and abilities. Join a team in a league that is best for you. An activity should allow you to perform at your peak potential. Mihály Csíkszentmihályi in his (1991) book, *Flow: The Psychology of Optimal Experience* explains that your level of skill must meet the level of challenge in order to have the best experience possible. Here is an example: if you participate in an activity that is too easy, you could feel "boredom." If the activity challenge is too great then you could feel "frustrated and overwhelmed."

An easy, free exercise you can do anywhere

I'd argue that simply walking is the easiest, most affordable physical fitness activity that a person could do. Buying a good pair of walking shoes would be the only cost for walking. Other costs could include buying an ipod so you'll be able to listen to energizing and motivating music while you walk. You may want to carry a cell phone for safety in case of an emergency, too. Otherwise, walking is free.

Make it exciting. Walk at various places opposed to the same 'ol dull routine. You could walk at your local park or a park in a neighboring city. Consider a hiking trail. Walk around the track at your local college or high school when it isn't in use. You could walk around the block of your neighborhood if it is safe and appropriate. You could walk laps around your mall.

I personally enjoy walking. It is an activity that calms my soul. I do walk at a pace to get exercise from it. Sometimes, I'll just take a leisurely walk where I'm mindful of the leaves, clouds, sunset, and flowers. I personally enjoy walking on a dull, grey day that has a light misty rain. Nature is quite then. Very few people are outside. I'll come back home, take a warm shower, and then drink hot mint-green tea while reading a good book. Walking allows you to take time to reflect on your life, what you have become, and what goals you want to work toward, too.

Eat healthy

Energy comes from food. You've got to eat the right foods. This is vital. You've got to get the right nutrients so that you can maintain health. You won't be able to do great things if you're in poor health. Protection from many disease and illnesses can come from eating the right foods. Many health problems are a direct result of poor eating habits. Eating poorly can have not-so-good consequences on your body. Eating right can result in a better immune system, more energy and having a healthier body weight.

You probably already know this information. I'm giving it here as a friendly reminder:

- Eat the right amount of foods from each food group.

- Mini-meals are better than larger meals. Several mini-meals opposed to three larger meals can help you to decrease calorie intake. You'll be able to burn off these calories through physical activity during the between times.

- Eat smaller portion meals opposed to large, heavy meals. Satisfy your hunger opposed to overindulgence. Eat until you feel almost full because the brain takes a little time to process all that you've eaten. You'll feel filled in a little while even if you still felt hungry before you finished eating.

- Fruits and veggies are the keys for snacks. You could learn that you like these. Try blueberries, blackberries, apples, carrots, celery, and other foods for snacks.

Avoid sedentary activities

Wasting time is never good. Do physical activities opposed to sedentary activities like watching television or playing video games.

Dad jumped on my brother and me once when we were in elementary school and I haven't forgotten the lesson. It was a beautiful summer day. My father had taken my sister to softball practice, which he helped coach. She was outdoors having a good time. My mother had mowed grass and walked around the neighborhood. They were all outdoors on this beautiful day. My brother (Jimmy) and I played a video game with two of our best friends, Chris and Chad. I still remember the game. It was called *Lemmings*. The game was very addictive. We sat there all evening right until dark playing that game. Dad came home and realized that we hadn't even left the television screen the whole time he had been gone with my sister for softball practice. He said that it was a waste of a good, beautiful day. Now that I think back, I realize that he was absolutely right. Sitting indoors playing video games isn't the best use of my time. I could have been using it to do something outdoors, like skateboarding (when I was younger) or doing something physical. I encourage you to remember this lesson, too. Do a physical activity outdoors.

Of course, there will be times when you're not participating in activities that are physically active, which are still good for you. These activities could be reading, writing, or doing other projects that you are working on for your personal growth and development. These activities are mentally active and stimulating, but not in a physical sense. My recommendation is to make sure that you also do physical fitness activities, too.

Avoid drugs and alcohol

Illness is the outcome for drinking, smoking, and doing drugs. In the long run a person will only suffer poor health from these things. Scientific studies have given enough proof to this. You don't need me to tell you.

I regret to say that I never had the opportunity to get to know either of my two biological grandfathers: (Posey Pettry) and (Raymond Keesee). Posey had died before I was born. Raymond had died when I was one-years-old. As a result, I never got to know them. I did know both of my grandmothers (Carrie Phillips Pettry Napier) and (Donna Keffer Graham Keesee). Both of grandmothers lived until the 2000s. My grandfather Posey had been a smoker and my grandfather Raymond had been a smoker and a drinker. I think these habits led to their earlier death. I feel certain that they could have had many more years of life had they made healthier choices. I would have had the opportunity to get to know them and learn from them.

Sleep well

Energy is one result of getting a good night sleep. Poor sleep can result in you feeling tired, stressed, and overwhelmed. You must get enough sleep if you want to become great.

Six to eight hours a night is recommended for sleeping. Schedule this time into your daily planner. Get in a habit of going to bed at the same time each night. Start to do calming activities at night an hour before going to bed. Turn off the television, turn off lights, do something relaxing. Doing a 30-minute workout or exercises will get your heart pumping and get your body all worked up. It is best not to do exercises right before bed. Avoid caffeine during the evening as well because it can prevent you from sleeping well.

Dream

Rapid-eye-movement (REM) sleep is what you're aiming for at night. This is the most productive sleep. It comes after a phase of light sleep and deep sleep. The REM period is when you dream. A person who doesn't get REM sleep is at risk for other health problems. It is vital that you sleep well so that you can achieve REM sleep. You'll know if you're getting this if you're dreaming. You may dream at night and not realize it. Getting a good night rest can help you to do many other great things during the day.

Taking care of your overall health and wellness will give you a longer life and more days of opportunity to do great things in life. If you want to be great then live healthy. Make good eating and exercise habits. Avoid habits that could end your life early. You could start today to make better choices for your life. You could eat a little better. You could do a little more physical activity. You could do a lot to improve your life.

The Hidden Secret Revealed in Chapter 11:

Taking care of your overall health and wellness will give you a longer life and more days of opportunity to do great things.

*** Upcoming Attraction ***

You could be lacking motivation to start making your life great. If so, continue reading to the next chapter because it is all about motivation techniques.

Chapter 11 References

Csíkszentmihályi, M. (1991). *The psychology of optimal experience.* Harper Perennial

Chapter 12

How to Use Your Potential Energy and Start Becoming Great with Motivation Techniques

"Go for it now.
The future is promised to no one."

- Wayne W. Dyer

Motivation

Passion for doing something has a special quality. It's motivation. When you have a desire to go out and do something you're feeling motivated. People have many different emotions. They could feel motivated or un-motivated. Emotion is also known as energy (E) in motion or E-motion. Motivation is a strong emotion because it gets you moving in the right direction. It helps you to accomplishing something great. It helps you to do all the wonderful things that you want to do in life.

Motivation is the willingness to do something. A person who is un-motivated does not have the desire to do something. She (or he) simply lacks the willingness to do whatever it is. You may lack motivation in some areas of your life. You may not want to clean house, do your push-ups, start a big project, go back to school, ask someone on a date, or so many other things. Motivation is the answer!

You could be wondering how you can motivate yourself to take action. The answer is to follow your passion. It is easy to get up and do something you love. Real motivation comes from the inside. This is the secret to getting things done. Internal motivation, according to Edward Deci and Richard Flaste in their (1996) book, *Why We Do What We Do: Understanding Self-Motivation,* is:

> "Doing an activity for its own sake for the rewards are inherit in the activity."

Alfie Kohn in his (2001) book, *Punished by Rewards: The Trouble with Gold Stars, Incentive Plans, A's, Praise, and Other Bribes,* argues that "external motivators are a poor substitute for internal motivators." In other words, using rewards such as money, candy, or other items will never be a strong of a motivator as the internal motivator. This is true because once the external reward ends, the behavior will stop. I've witnessed this myself working with children. Some therapists develop elaborate behavior-modification plans to get children to change behaviors. The child is rewarded a "10-minute playtime" for demonstrating a certain behavior for two hours. After a week, the therapist will change it to four hours, six hours, or eight hours. As you guessed, the behavior goes back to normal once the rewards are lessened. Sometimes it backfires. The child will act worse and say that they need to have a reward every two hours again so that they'll behave. The child is attempting to control the therapist and use her aggressive behavior in order to get a reward more often.

Believe in possibilities

Faith is the key ingredient for motivation. You must believe that it is possible. People who think it isn't possible simply won't try. They've already got it in their minds that anything they do won't work. The person who thinks there might be a chance will go ahead and act on it. As a result, they're more likely to achieve it because they are taking action. Wayne Gretzky (retired Canadian professional ice hockey player) said: "you'll miss 100% of the chances you never take."

Possibilities are endless. Many people have done things that have seemed impossible. People have built pyramids, flew planes, harnessed electricity, created the internet, and so much more. It's hard to imagine what the future will be like because there are so many creative people out there like you. You've got amazing talents to offer this world. Things we think are big today, like the internet, ipods, and blackberries will be outdated in the future. They'll be like black-and-white television set, 8-track-tapes, and a rotary dial telephones. All of these were the leading technology at one time. Your creative actions are going to make this world a better place if you take action.

I personally enjoy studying people who came from a disadvantage and have accomplished great things in their lives. I almost think that being born at a disadvantage is a far greater advantage opposed to being born with everything. The person who has been given it all does not learn how to go out to work and make things happen.

Here are three examples of people who I admire who've come from disadvantage, or had some type of shortcoming who were discussed earlier in this book:

- Harry Truman was born on a small farm in Missouri. He was poor. He became one of the greatest Presidents of the United States and my personal favorite.

- Bethany Hamilton lost an arm in a rare shark attack, but she is winning surfing contests with one arm.

- Shea Cowart is a track star. She has won gold medals. Shea had Meningococcal disease as a child and became an amputee at the age of 6, but she still runs.

Here is one more example of a person who has overcome obstacles:

- Logan is the creative director of *Logan Magazine*. It is an excellent and inspirational magazine for youth with disabilities. Logan had a brain injury at the age of 16, which left her with limited mobility. She still followed her dreams by being the creative director of a leading magazine. I highly recommend *Logan Magazine* for people without disabilities because it features stories of successful people who are overcoming obstacles. It is great for motivation. For more information, go online: http://www.loganmagazine.com

What is holding you back if people like Bethany, Shea, and Logan are doing great things? With or without a disability, you can do great things with your life. You can become great.

What is it that you really want to do?

Think back to what you learned about yourself from the first chapter in this book (on self-discovery). If you really want to do it then the motivation will be there already. You won't need me to talk you into doing it.

I really wanted to write a book. Writing didn't require any extra persuasion. I want to stay in shape and live long, so I eat right and walk daily. I want to be a do-gooder, so I donate blood, recycle, give to charity, and work in the human services profession.

Use visualization

Pictures are said to be worth a 1,000 words. There are plenty of pictures stored away in your mind. You've got images and visualizations of great things. I recommend that you take time to dream and visualize what it is that you want to have, do, or be in life. Visualize it to be as real as possible. Use all of your senses in your imagination. What does it feel like? What does it taste like? What does it smell like? What do you hear? What do you see? Are there any other feelings?

Writing this great self-improvement book was my goal. Visualization helped make this book a reality. Proof of that is evident in that you're holding the book in your hands and reading it right now. Here is what I did: I created a fake cover of the book. I posted it by my computer so that I could visualize the book daily. I daydreamed about signing my autograph to books. I even practiced signing autographs a few times by just signing my name to the front page of my personal books. I could hear people saying, "Wow, you've written a book" and "You're an author?" These are strong visualization techniques that work. I visualized myself doing what I wanted until it became real. I visualized you reading my book. I saw you discovering hidden secret wisdom and being inspired to take action to accomplish things in your life.

Creative Visualization: Use the Power of Your Imagination to Create What You Want in Your Life by Shakti Gawain is one of my favorite books. It was originally published in 1978, two years before I was even born. Gawain shares tips on how to use your mind to have greater personal growth, development, and satisfaction. You've got to put *Creative Visualization* on your list of books to read. It is inspirational and easy-to-read.

I think Gawain's book should be on the reading list for children in elementary school. School teaches our children how to read, write, do math, and a few other things. School doesn't teach children vital skills such as self-awareness, personal growth and development, self-esteem, stress management, social interaction skills, and of course, creative visualization. Which curriculum do you think a child would become more successful as the result of taking?

My brother, Jimmy, asked what exactly do I do as a recreational therapist earlier this year. I replied that I teach valuable skills to children, including: social interaction skills, goal planning, stress management, leisure education, self-esteem, and life management skills through the use of recreation, education, and treatment activities. Jimmy replied, "They've got an advantage over kids in public school [because public school doesn't offer these courses]. Take time to teach yourself these things by reading good books.

Ken Robinson (2009) in his book, *The Element*, said that a young girl, Gillian went to dance school as a child and as a result she performed better in all of her other subjects. It gives you something to think about. Gillian was the kind of kid who learned from body movement (a.k.a. kinesiology). Her mind had to work to learn the dance moves, steps, and rhythm.

Two minds are smarter than one

Networking and people skills were the main subject of chapter nine in this book. Napoleon Hill, in his classic, (1937) book, *Think and Grow Rich,* argued that a person needed a "mastermind group" in order to become successful. This is a group of people who get together to share ideas and support each other. The most successful people have a mastermind group. They are like secret societies. Motivational speaker, Jim Rohn in his (2000) *Jim Rohn Sampler* CD, argues that a millionaire should try inviting a billionaire to the group. Rohn is making it evident that millionaires must have billionaires in their "mastermind group" in order to become billionaires. If you've not done so already, read Hill's classic, *Think and Grow Rich* book.

Here is how I used a mastermind group to help me with this book. I developed connections with experts to help me along the path. I made partnerships with people while I was still writing this book. This further encouraged me to stick with the writing process. I couldn't back out of the book once I had partnerships. My complete mastermind group is listed in the acknowledgements section at the front of this book. I wouldn't have had a successful book without their help.

Don't tell the nay-sayers

Jealous people will try to stop you from going for your dreams. They will say put-downs and other comments to discourage you. Don't tell them your hopes and dreams. Share your desires and visions with your secret mastermind group only. Your group of inspirational people will inspire you. Nay-sayers will try to rain on your parade. Dale Carnegie in his (1936) classic book, *How to Win Friends and Influence People,* would say these are the people who "criticize, condemn, and complain."

In 2007, I wanted to start an online continuing education program for recreational therapists and allied professionals. I didn't tell several close people in my life that I was going to start a business. I knew they would discourage it. They would tell me it was a waste of time and money. They would say it wasn't worth it.

I knew it was worth it. I wanted to do it because it was important to me and many people who would use my services. So, I didn't tell the nay-sayers. I took a business class in January of 2007. I was the founding member of a mastermind group, called, (The Huntington Business Force), which I served as the 2nd president. I studied and read about business concepts, marketing, and online sales. I interviewed people who were already in business.

I created a business plan and developed, *Independent Education for the Recreational Therapist.* It is a Limited Liability Company (LLC) that is based out of West Virginia that provides recreational therapists and allied professionals worldwide with self-study courses for continuing education.

My website is: www.DannyPettry.Com

It is a successful small business. People from nearly every state in America have taken courses, including people from Puerto Rico and the District of Columbia. People from Canada and New Zealand have taken courses, too. I am getting the opportunity to help serve fellow recreational therapists around the world and I enjoy doing it. I love meeting students who take my courses.

I had a vision to create a business and I didn't tell people who would discourage me. Then one day, I said to the Nay-sayers, guess what I've been doing? I'm running a worldwide education and training business. Do you want to see my website?

It was already a success before they had the opportunity to say I shouldn't do it. Of course, as with any business, it has its ups and downs. It requires hard work. I have put in more work than what I receive back monetary. But it pays off in other ways. I do make profit and I enjoy doing it.

Set a Deadline

Deadlines get people moving. They are vital to motivation. You'll see it in sales ads all the time. (Here is an example, this coupon or discount ends by such and such date so act now. Hurry before it's too late).

I worked at *Chick-fil-A*, a fast-food restaurant that serves delicious chicken sandwiches. They used deadlines to motivate employees to serve fast. All the computer screens have a timer for each order. We were expected to get the order to the customer in one-minute. After 60 seconds, the timer on the screen turns red, starting at 1:01.

Chick-fil-A (of Beckley, West Virginia) had a contest during one Christmas holiday season. Our boss said that the first person who can ring up $1,000 dollars on a single register will get a permanent 25 cent raise an hour. That inspired me. I began to work extra fast. Two people did it and we both got the raise. I am proud to say that I was the first person to do it. The deadline worked because I knew I had to do it before the end of the season. My co-worker, Angela had also got this raise. Opportunity to ring up this amount in sales was most likely possible during the holiday rush. I knew I had until Jan. 1st to do it. I did it on Black Friday in November. There were six cashiers working at the same time. Anyone could have done it. I just stayed at my register and continued to serve people. Here is another secret. I made good friends with mall employees. I was always extra "smiley and friendly." Some mall employees would avoid short lines and purposely wait in my line just so that I could serve them. This probably contributed to my success.

Earlier in this book, I told you that I am opposed to external rewards. Getting a 25-cent raise is an external reward. Would a person continue working hard without the reward? The external reward for being a good employee wasn't the primary motivator. I did it because I was internally motivated to "be a good employee." Hard-work is one of my personal values.

Motivation does not last if you're only doing it for the money. You've got to do it for an internal desire. I earned a 25-cent raise per hour as a result of hard work at *Chick-fil-A*. That was a big raise because most people got a nickel extra an hour added to their salary once per year.

I continued to do my best at *Chick-fil-A* because I knew I wanted to be a good worker. I wanted to provide a good service to people who ate at the restaurant. I wanted to learn all that I could from the job. I wanted to build skills that would prepare me for my next job. I didn't work hard to make an extra quarter an hour. I worked hard to make myself a more valuable person.

Warning: A person who is strongly motivated by external rewards such as money may find other non-productive ways to get their external rewards. Based on my experiences working with children, they'll learn to become sneakier. They'll get rewarded for their "not-being-caught doing the behavior." It creates more sneakiness, lying, cheating, and stealing in order to get the reward. In the long-run, a person highly motivated by rewards could develop inappropriate habits. Here is an example: Stealing and selling drugs, although illegal, could result in a prize, a lot of money, fast.

Focusing on "money" as a reward seems like a poor idea. I'm certain I could make better money doing a lot of other things. I've seen a posting for a manager position at a *Starbucks* coffee shop that paid more than my recreational therapist salary. If rewards were true motives, then I would have left a long time ago. I do my job because of the internal desire to help people. I love what I do and I couldn't see myself doing anything else. It would be very difficult for me to leave my job.

Obtaining a national certification to practice recreational therapy and completing a master's degree in recreational therapy were great accomplishments. I feel proud of doing these things. It took a lot of time and money. I was rewarded more responsibilities at work as a result of it. My employers didn't offer a raise for certification or advanced degrees. One of my supervisors said that I had "hurt myself because certification and a graduate degree were not required." I felt very bitter about that comment for a while. I finally learned to forgive and let it go. I feel that it will pay off in the long run. It pays off now in that I am providing a higher quality of services to my patients. We live in a world of change. Healthcare is rapidly changing. People want healthcare services that work. Recreational therapists who are trained will be better prepared to bring about effective outcomes and positive changes in people who they serve.

The secret: learn all that you can. Obtain all the knowledge, skills, and abilities that you are capable of.

Mission

Mission statements were a concept that I learned about when I read Sean Covey's (1998) book, *The 7 Habits of Highly Effective Teens.* Covey recommended that the reader should create a personal mission statement. He compares it to a big business. They have purposes and mission statements. Here is some good news: Your mission statement can change over the years, too. I created my first mission statement in 2000 after I had read Covey's book. It read that I would complete a degree in therapeutic recreation from Marshall University by 2002. It read that I would become a recreational therapist after graduation. Covey's technique worked. I did both of these things. I was very worried that I wouldn't find employment after graduation. I sent resumes and applications to hospitals in both Virginias and Carolinas. I only had two interviews. Amazingly, I graduated on Aug. 12, 2002 from Marshall and had my first two job interviews on Aug. 12th after giving my final presentation on the summer internship in recreation therapy. I began my first day of work as a recreational therapist on Aug. 13, 2002. Naturally, I had to re-write my mission statement then because I had achieved my goals. I had to develop a newer, more long-term vision.

Don't make the mistake that I did. Be sure to include all areas on your mission statement. My former college mission statement only included education and career. Your mission statement should also discuss your significant other, family and friends, spirituality, and of course you hobbies and leisure interests.

Today, my mission statement reads:

"To be the greatest healer in the world. I want to do all that I can to make the world a better place to live in both professionally and personally. I will marry a pretty woman, have children, and live in a nice home before I'm 35. I will be a good man who takes care of them. I will support them financially. I will continually partake in self-improvement and personal development to learn all that I can in life as well as to teach and give all the love that I can. I'll write a novel before the end of 2010."

Revised January 1, 2009.
This is to be revised again on Jan. 1, 2010

Signed: *Danny W. Pettry, II*

Let me know how I'm doing. I believe this book is part of my mission in making the world a better place.

You can sign-up to receive my FREE Wisdom Revealed e-Newsletter. It provides book summaries on inspirational, motivational, and useful books. It's my way of showing love and teaching all the wisdom that I've learned.
Go here: www.HiddenSecretWisdom.Com

Remember the magic number

Ten-thousand (10,000) is the magic number. Malcom Gladwell in his (2008) book, *Outliers, the Story of Success*, said that "10,000" is the number of hours that it takes in order to be great at something. It takes years of hard work, practice, and dedication to be the best. That is a lot of time. <u>You've got to start to take action today.</u>

Real success does not happen overnight. The younger a person, the more hours of practice she'll have already put in towards becoming great.

The best of the best have been dedicated. They've put in their 10,000 hours of hard work at their talent. Take Larry Bird, one of the best NBA basketball players of all-time for an example. Larry Bird's high school basketball coach, Jim Jones, said: "Bird would always be in the gym early, shoot in between classes, and then stay late into the evening. He quit both football and baseball to focus on the sport he loved, basketball (Wikipedia, 2009)." If is obvious that Bird started at an early age putting in hours of practice in order to be the best at basketball. The list of professionals who have put in their time is endless.

People with the most practice are going to be best. Start today by putting in your time, dedication, and effort into activities that you find meaningful.

An old Chinese proverb reads:

> "A journey of 1,000 miles starts with a single step."
>
> **- Confucius**

You must take your first step towards your goal today. Another Chinese proverb reads:

> "It's not the destination that is important.
> It's the journey."

Enjoy the process. Be happy with the now. Read good books along the way to help you stay motivated and dedicated.

> "People often say that motivation doesn't last. Well, neither does bathing that's why we recommend it daily."
>
> **- Zig Ziglar**

> **The Hidden Secret Revealed in Chapter 12:**
>
> *Take Action.*
> *Do Something Wonderful with Your Life.*

Your Free Bonuses for Buying this Book!

You can download and print the following e-book:

Bonus # 1

Wisdom Revealed:
The Complimentary Journal on Becoming Great

It is available exclusively for you at this link online:

www.HiddenSecretWisdom.com/bonus

30+ More Bonuses

You're entitled to get 30+ more bonuses as my gift to you for buying this book. These gifts include e-books, articles on success and achievement, and more. They're written by some of the leading experts from around the world. This is a growing list. More articles will be added to help you on your quest to become the best.

These are available exclusively for you at this link online:

www.HiddenSecretWisdom.com/bonus

Conclusion

In my personal opinion, the # 1 skill needed for becoming great is *literacy*. People need to know how to read and write in order to become successful. A person must actively read books throughout their lifespan to discover all the secret knowledge that one can obtain. *You've Got to Read This Book!: 55 People Tell the Story of the Book That Changed Their Life* by Jack Canfield and Gay Hendricks (2006) could be a good starting guide for must-read books.

Jack Canfield discussed an interesting book, called, *Life After Life: The Investigation of a Phenomenon--Survival of Bodily Death* by Dr. Raymond Moody in his (2006) book, *You've Got to Read This Book!* Dr. Moody studied people who had been pronounced "dead," but had returned to life. Dr. Moody believes that there is life on the other side based on his interviews.

Canfield (2006) said that one interviewee's comments from Dr. Moody's book had deeply inspired him. The interviewee reported being asked two questions in the afterlife. These questions were:

"What wisdom have you gained from this life?

How have you expanded your capacity to love?"

These two questions could give you something to think about. Learn all that you can and love in all ways that you can.

Hidden, secret wisdom can be found in books, but you've got to read them to discover wisdom. Read all that you can. Learn all the wisdom that you can.

Attention Parents: Fill your house with books that are age appropriate for kids. This could create the learning environment to encourage your child to be a lifelong reader. Imitate the reading habit by reading to your children. Start today if you don't do this already.

Finally, be a "Do-Gooder," and make this world a better place. Love all people and share your good-will and wisdom with others.

Here is a quick review of all the chapters:

Chapter One: Who Else Wants to Discover the First Step to Becoming Great? Here is the first step:

Know who you are and what you want

Chapter Two: This is the Most Powerful Tool Used for Self-Development and Personal Growth:

Use a success journal to become great

Chapter Three: At Last! Here's How to Discover Hidden Secret Wisdom for Becoming Great.
Do this:

> Read a book a week, at least

Chapter Four: Discover What Successful People Already Know about Becoming Great? Do this:

> Learn wisdom from studying great people

Chapter Five: The Truth About Teachers And Why You Need One to Become Great:

> Get a personal teacher, coach, or mentor as soon as possible because they can show you the way to becoming great

Chapter Six: These Movies Inspire Greatness in About 90-Minutes-A-Day:

> Learn secrets to become great by watching inspirational, life-changing, movies and documentaries

Chapter Seven: New Discovery Reveals How Being Happy Will Help You to Become Great!

> You must feel happy most of the time before you can become great

Chapter Eight: Here's How To Become Great In Your Spare Time - And Have Fun Doing It!

> Start participating in activities that you are passionate about doing because you're more likely to become great at things you enjoy

Chapter Nine: Here's The Best Way to Become Great, Get a Job, or Do Anything:

> Develop people skills. Know no stranger. Create a strong social support network. You'll need people

Chapter Ten: Why Do-Gooders are More Likely to Become Great and Successful:

> Help make this world a better and greater place. Give to people in need. It could help you to discover your real passion or calling in life

Chapter Eleven: A Health and Fitness Program Can Help You to Become Great... Guaranteed!

> You won't be able to do anything if you're not taking care of yourself

Chapter Twelve: How to Use Your Potential Energy and Start Becoming Great with Motivation Techniques:

> Just take action. Start to do something wonderful with your life right now.

Now What?

Download your free bonuses. They're available exclusively for you here:

> www.hiddensecretwisdom.com/bonus

I hope you've been inspired by this book to start reading, learning, and loving. Email me with your comments. Danny@dannypettry.com

Yours truly,

Danny Wayne Pettry II.

Danny Wayne Pettry, II, MS, CTRS
Recreational Therapist & Humanitarian

Chapter 12 and Conclusion References

Canfield, J. (2006). *You've Got to Read This Book!: 55 People Tell the Story of the Book That Changed Their Life.* New York: HarperCollins.
Deci, E., & Flaste, R. (1996). *Why We Do What We Do: Understanding Self-Motivation.* Boston: Penguin.
Gawain, S. (2002). *Creative Visualization: Use the Power of Your Imagination to Create What You Want in Your Life.* Novato: New World Library.
Gladwell, M. (2008). *Outliers: The Story of Success.* Boston: Little, Brown.
Kohn, A. (2001). *Punished by Rewards: The Trouble with Gold Stars, Incentive Plans, A's, & Praise.* Chicago: Replica Books.
Moody, R. (2001). *Life After Life: The Investigation of a Phenomenon--Survival of Bodily Death.* SanFrancisco: HarperCollins.
Robinson, K. (2009). *The Element: How Finding Your Passion Changes Everything.* New York: Viking Adult.
Rohn, J. (2000). *Jim Rohn sampler.* [compact disc]. Dallas: Jim Rohn International.

Need Continuing Education Credits?

Danny Pettry's Independent Education for the Recreational Therapist, LLC strives to be the # 1 self-study continuing education program online for recreational therapists and allied professionals.

You can complete self-study courses in three easy steps. First, you read an interesting book. Second, you pass a multiple choice quiz online to demonstrate that you have a basic understanding of the knowledge area. You're guaranteed to pass or you can re-take the quiz. Finally, you can print your certificate upon completion. You can implement your new-gained knowledge and skills into your practice.

Try one of Danny Pettry's amazing self-study courses. They're affordable, accessible, flexible, and easy-to-complete.

Go online: http://www.DannyPettry.Com

You have access to a FREE 5-clock-hour self-study course as a bonus gift for buying this book. It's called: ***Professional Development in Recreational Therapy***. It includes techniques for becoming the best recreational therapist that you can be. Access your free course at the link below. It's bonus #29.

http://www.hiddensecretwisdom.com/bonus

Danny is an approved provider of continuing education for RNs. **Provider #: WV 2007-0520RN.** As with any continuing education program, The National Council for Therapeutic Recreation Certification (NCTRC) does not pre-approve any continuing education activities.

Please tell your family, friends, or co-workers to get a copy of this book, too!

Reminder: It's not about the book. It's about the mission. The goal of *Discover Hidden Secret Wisdom* is to promote the #1 skill needed to become great. Danny Pettry believes that skill is ***literacy.*** Books are filled with wisdom that you won't discover unless you read them. Many children in the world do not live in homes with age-appropriate books for them to read.

A portion of the profits made from this book will benefit the non-profit First Book.

First Book provides new books to children in need addressing one of the most important factors affecting literacy – access to books.

Who is Danny Pettry, II?

Mr. Danny Pettry, II

Danny Pettry, II, is a Recreational Therapist. He has held Certified Therapeutic Recreation Specialist (CTRS) credentials since 2003. He earned a Master of Science degree in Therapeutic Recreation from Indiana University, Bloomington, Indiana in 2006. He earned a Bachelor of Science degree in Park Resources and Leisure Services with a focus in Therapeutic Recreation from Marshall University, Huntington, West Virginia in 2002. Danny has provided recreational therapy services at a residential treatment facility located in one of the two Virginias since 2002 for children between the ages of 7 and 13 who are abuse-reactive. These children have suffered physical, sexual, and/ or emotional abuse, and/ or severe neglect and have learned to act out the same abusive behaviors on others. Danny enjoys helping these kids. He provides a mix of treatment interventions to help these children to develop social interaction skills, empathy for others, self-worth, calming skills, problem-solving skills, and basic life skills. He also provides recreation services to maintain and promote their overall wellbeing and quality of life while being a resident at the treatment facility.

Danny has been a good-standing member of the American Therapeutic Recreation Association (ATRA) since 2000. He was acknowledged as a "Recreational Therapy Advocate of the Year" in 2005 by ATRA. He had won the ATRA - Dr. Peg Connolly Student Scholarship to the national conference in Kansas City, Missouri in 2004.

Danny Pettry's Family

Danny was born and raised in Beckley, West Virginia. He is the son of Danny Pettry (senior) and Teresa Keesee-Pettry. He grew up with his brother, Jimmy, and sister, Carrie. They are all good people who live good lives.

Danny Pettry (senior) graduated from (the former Morris Harvey College), which is now University of Charleston in West Virginia. He completed a Master of Arts degree from the West Virginia College of Graduate Studies, which is now part of Marshall University. He began teaching and has been a principal since the 70s. He has been the school principal at Crescent Elementary School of Beckley, West Virginia since 1989. It's a National Blue Ribbon – No Child Left Behind (NCLB) School of Excellence. He is a hard worker and a good father. He has been married to, Teresa, since 1975.

Teresa Keesee Pettry graduated from Woodrow Wilson High School. She is a caring and loving mother. She has always done everything she can for her family. Her list of jobs is endless. They include: laundry, ironing, dishes, vacuuming, cleaning, rearing the children, helping with homework, babysitting other children, caretaking for in-laws during their elderly years, babysitting her grandson, Gage, and then, more laundry. She is a good person.

Jimmy Pettry graduated from Woodrow Wilson High School and Concord University. He is a computer specialist for Greenbrier County, WV - Board of Education. He married his high school girlfriend, **Emily Hartling**. They have one son, **Gage Christopher Pettry**.

Carrie Pettry graduated from Woodrow Wilson High School and the Academy of Careers and Technology. She is a phlebotomist. Carrie loves animals, especially cats.

54835645R00129

Made in the USA
San Bernardino, CA
24 October 2017